How to pray the Word of God

Prayer Declarations

Mantsha Pheeha

Website	http://www.mantsha.com
email	Mantsha@mantsha.com
LInkedin	Mantsha Pheeha
facebook	mantsha.com
Twitter	@mantsha
Instagram	Mantsha Pheeha
You tube	Mantsha Pheeha

All Scripture quotations are taken from the New King James Version and where a different version is used, it will be indicated in the text.

ISBN-13: 9798614955236
ISBN-10: 1512211966

DEDICATION

To every believer who desires to pray according to the Word of God.

This book is dedicated to my mother Ngwakwana Ruth Pheeha nee' Masekela and my father Matome Patrick "The Fish" Pheeha for always believing in me.

PRAISE FOR HOW TO PRAY THE WORD

This book will help remove a burden so many of us often feel in prayer on what we need to say in order to make our prayer effective. The greatest strength of this book is Pastor Mantsha's unrelenting emphasis that prayer cannot be an add-on to the Christian life. Prayer is instead: an active practice or lifestyle of tearing down strongholds by captivating our minds with the knowledge of God . A thematic scriptural underpinning approach presented in prayer form, incorporated into declaratory daily prayer life as a way of letting God's Word take centre stage. This provides a firm foundation instrumental in equipping the saints through prayer and confession of the Word of God. How to pray the Word of God gives me such comfort and freedom knowing that I am more inclined to pray God's will into my situations. This book is a Must Read.

Apostle Jack T. Tsoai
Visionary & Leader of Capstone Translocal Partnerships

We live in a fast-paced world where things are constantly evolving. More often than not we are just focused on trying to silence the 'noise' of the many things which require our attention daily. At the same time, we constantly have to find renewed strength and hope to live abundantly. There are so many "solutions" which are offered as a recipe for a balanced life, and yet often they miss the basics. This book takes us back to the basics through prayer. The declarations are easy and effective in helping one refocus their energy, change their perspective about life and speak light into every situation.

Cathy Mohlahlana
News Anchor & Motivational Speaker

How to pray the Word of God is a must-read, it teaches you as a child of God how to pray using the Bible. It covers most areas of an individual's life. It encourages me to go study the Word of God and to hear what He has promised about my life. As a married person I am taught through the Word of God to be like God and speak life in my marriage and family. Through the declarations I speak what i want to see in my marriage and in my child's life. I am taught to look at life through the eyes of God and not according to my situation. In the beginning God spoke all things into being and I am reminded in the book that as I am made in the image of God I need to be like He is and speak things into being in my life according to His Word.

Mokgadi Mahlangu
Mother, Wife & Teacher

Ps Mantsha is my friend. I have known her since 1996 and I know what she has written in this book is how she has always wanted us as Christians to be aligned with the word of God. The book you are holding may be one of the best books you will ever read. It is a book meant to align your way of life with the word of God. It will help you translate God's promises to personal experiences and victories. Through this book, Ps Mantsha has put a structured approach to our daily challenge of aligning our thoughts, prayers and confessions with the Word of God. I encourage you to look at this book more as a tool and a daily companion as you walk through your own journey. The promises of God are yes and amen. Ps Mantsha has written a book to help all of us experience these promises as yes and amen at a personal level.

Bohani Hlungwane (MBA)
Senior Global Banker
Senior Executive Leadership Program at Stanford University
Bachelor of Commerce Honours in Financial & Monetary Economics
Bachelor of Commerce in Economics

How to pray the Word of God

CONTENTS

FOREWORD

This book is a culmination of years of developing, arranging and leading word-based declarations at the annual January and Easter conventions of the Change Bible church in Katlehong. The January convention is the biggest annual event hosted by the church. This event is attended by thousands of Christians from all over the country and it sets the tone and direction for the year. Arranging and leading declarations at these services lifts the spirit and the mind of the church for the year ahead. This has resulted in numerous requests for Pastor Mantsha to share these declarations with guests and other churches.

I have witnessed Pastor Mantsha lead and inspire the thousands who attend the services, invigorate and encourage them to keep believing. This book was written to ensure that even those who may not have attended the conventions may also benefit from these word-based declarations and be able to share them with their friends, families and even declare them during their church services or at home.

This book will lead you to a point of believing again if you were in doubt and it will show you word-based declarations which if made in earnest will completely transform your prayer life and your life. The pages of this book are filled with wisdom in its simple form. It is not the good grammar and the inspirational phrases that will grab you, but the word mixed with faith and revealed by the Spirit of God that will move you to your next level of your faith.

Whatever your need is, this book is for you. The author has gone to great lengths to search the scriptures relevant to each topic and share them with you, the reader. This is to ensure that whichever declaration you make is based on scripture, as the bible says God is looking to perform His word. We therefore cannot declare and hold God to anything which is not based on His word. Most of us need healing and maybe we have been taught to stand in a queue on Sunday or during a healing service to obtain healing. This book teaches a Christian to take God at His word and declare healing without having to attend a service.

The Author, Mantsha Pheeha, is a pastor and she has been involved in ministry for the past 20 years. I have the privilege of watching Mantsha go about her business of spreading the message of the Kingdom, within her local church and beyond and it is a great picture to see. How she has managed to cover her greatness with humility and kindness is amazing. How she meticulously interprets and explains the word of God to help the church of Jesus Christ to move to the next level is wisdom and simplicity personified. This book is no exception.

As a professional, a pastor and a minister of the gospel for over 20 years, I have read and gone through hundreds of Christian, motivational and self-help books. This book is one of the simplest, word-based, and inspirational and life changing books I have read. It led me to a place where I just don't pray, but hold God to His word, more like read it back to Him.

Happy life-changing reading everyone

Pastor Hlohlo Moroeng (Deputy Business Executive, Auditor General of South Africa)

Senior Associate Pastor: Change Bible Church

Katlehong, South Africa

ACKNOWLEDGMENTS

How to pray the Word of God was born out of my responsibilities at Change Bible Church. I was tasked with developing and arranging declaration statements that were aligned to our convention themes, and thereafter leading the congregation in making these declarations during church services., This book was born out of those assignments. I would like to acknowledge Ps JX Nzo, the senior pastor of Change Bible Church, who entrusted me with the task of leading the declarations and for giving me the platform to minister. I would like to thank everyone who believed in me and kept encouraging me to share the declarations. This book would not have been possible without the Change family of churches.

I would like to thank Ps Hlohlo for countless input, additional content and for editing the book over and over again. Nomfundo Mcilongo, Cathy Mohlahlana, Ps Jack Tsoai, Bohani Hlungwane, Fanalo Mahlangu and Mokgadi Mahlangu for their input and Ngwako Ramohlale for her creative genius. I would also like to thank Yvonne Thiebaut for editing the manuscript.

The success of this book belongs to all of us.

1 PROLOGUE

"I am the head and not the tail!"
The crowd would be on their feet, shouting mostly with fists clenched in the air: "I am the head and not the tail!"
"I have been placed above only and not beneath!"
Once more, the thundering echo from the crowd could be heard, repeating after the person leading the declarations section of our services: "I have been placed above only and not beneath!"

We would then go on for the next ten minutes and end off with a shout and praise. The whole assembly, still on their feet, would continue praying on their own - some thanking God, others making petitions and intercessions to the Lord. The mood is set for prayer, we are ready to receive, and we are standing on the sure foundation of the Word of God.

For the past three years, I have been leading word-based declarations in our conference services and every year I am inundated with requests to share the declarations with conference attendees. This book is a response to those requests; it provides Christians with a tool that will help them inject the Word of God into their everyday prayers and regular speech.

For every Christian there are times when we all just need a little help to get started with prayer. Sometimes, as children of God, we want to pray the word but we just don't know where to start. These declarations are here to provide much needed help but they are not supposed to replace your prayer time. Prayer flows out of relationship and these declarations are just introductory statements to assist you to go deeper with God. Don't end here but seek a deeper and more intimate relationship with God. Ask the Holy Spirit to guide and lead you as you pray. Read them aloud, mix the word with faith and wait on God to meet you at the point of your need.

Gone are the days when we pray and just keep saying Fire…Fire…Fire! Now we graduate and we speak the word! Enjoy a word-filled time of prayer!

PS MANTSHA PHEEHA

2 HOW TO USE THIS BOOK

How to pray the Word of God is a book written to help every Christian to pray according to the bible. As Christians, we know that we are supposed to pray according to the bible but sometimes when we face difficult situations, we don't know where and how to start.

Section A of this book, Why We Need Prayer Declarations, provides the basis for prayer declarations. Section B, Prayer Declarations, outlines the declarations that a Christian can use for different situations.

Before you start using this book you are encouraged to spend some time reading Section A so that you can understand why it is important to confess the Word of God in your prayers. Once you have established the rationale for confessing the word, you are ready to continue to Section B, which outlines the actual prayer declarations.

This book is not supposed to be read like a novel and the goal for the reader should not be to quickly go through the book to the end. I propose that at first, you go through the whole book to familiarise yourself with the content. Once you have gone through the book for the first time, you can then identify topics that you would like to pray about and declare them out loud as you pray. Feel free to add your own declarations, the trick is that the declarations must be based on the Word of God, which simply means that you need a verse to back your declaration.

If you are praying or believing for something specific in your life or in the life of another, you can go to that topic and declare out loud and you can lead another person or a group in the declarations so that you can put the law of agreement in motion: Whatever two agree on, on earth, it shall be done for them.

SECTION A:
WHY WE NEED PRAYER DECLARATIONS?

3 CREATING WITH YOUR WORDS

In the beginning when God created the heavens and earth, the bible tells us that the earth was without form, it was void and that darkness was on the face of the deep. It's funny how the bible also mentions that the Spirit of the Lord was hovering over the face of the waters. For me, as a mortal human being, I would have thought that the Spirit of the Lord being there would mean that there was order in the situation. Often when we are saved, we assume that God will automatically make things work out for us and most of us are frustrated that our situations are not changing and yet we are dedicated to God and spending time in His presence. We associate the presence of God with order and immediate breakthrough.

The bible then tells us what God does as He is introduced to that situation. God immediately gets there and says: "Let there be light." God doesn't address the situation that he finds, he doesn't address the darkness, but instead he declares and speaks the thing He wants to see, which in this case, is the light. This theme remains throughout Genesis chapter one. God then spends the next day declaring in great detail what He wants to see on the earth. This is the portion of scripture known as creation, where God shows us how things are created. Light, Heaven, Earth, Seas, Grass, Trees, Herbs, the Moon, the Sun, the Stars, Living Creatures in the waters, Birds, Beasts of earth, Cattle and Creeping things were all created by God speaking them into being.

God spoke and whatever thing He said came into being. What He spoke became. From Genesis 1 verses 3 to 25, we are introduced to a God who speaks things into being. We meet a God who speaks and as soon as He speaks, whatever He says becomes. There is no concept of time, God just speaks, immediately it happens. He says it is good and moves on to the next thing. This is the God we know up to this point in verse 25.

In verse 26 God creates man, you and I, and unlike all the other times when He was creating He said: "Let Us make man in Our image, according to Our likeness." Just as He had done previously, the Bible then further confirms that "God created man in His own image; in the image of God He created him; male and female He created them. Then God blessed them, and God said to them, "Be fruitful and multiply; fill the earth and subdue it; have dominion over the fish of the sea, over the birds of the air, and over every living thing that moves on the earth."

History, and history in this case means from verses one to twenty five of Genesis, has already taught us a few things. Firstly, we already know that when God speaks anything into existence, it happens just as He said it. Secondly, we know by now that whatever God speaks happens immediately, there is no process and there is no time delay. Armed with these two pieces of information we can conclude, without a shadow of a doubt, that immediately man was created in the image and likeness of God. There is no process of becoming, as God said it, right at that moment we were in His image and according to His likeness. There is no debate about who we are. Just like God, when we desire anything we can now speak it into being and immediately it shall be just as we say it.

Most of us can argue that we have waited on God and there was a delay before we saw the manifestation of what we prayed for. This is where we pause and remind ourselves that: we understand by faith. The same faith that guarantees that you have the substance whilst you are still hoping; that faith is the proof, before you see with your eyes what you believe. It is also the faith that will bring you testimony and ensure that you please God. By faith we receive what we pray for before it appears in the physical realm.

We are creators, and we create with our mouths. We speak things into being, just like our God because we are made in His image and according to His likeness. God didn't address the situation by going to great lengths to describe the state of affairs, and that is exactly how we need to deal with every negative situation. We must move away from describing the sickness, the lack and poverty, the struggle and suffering in our lives but instead we must be like God and speak the healing, deliverance, salvation, and breakthrough that God has already given us. Creators must create and never complain. As we complain, we are creating what we don't want to see, we confirm the very situation we don't want to see.

God being God, the earth could have had form from the onset or God could have thought the things into existence, yet He spoke. He created with His words because He was demonstrating to us that we too, seeing we are made in His image, can create with our words. There is always the temptation to think our prayers or to just wish but the power of creation lies in us speaking things into being.

4 THE POWER OF YOUR WORDS

The bible teaches us about the importance of the words we speak and reminds us that words are not just a means of communication but they are the very building blocks that we use to create the life we have been made to live. Verses like Proverbs 18:20-21, tell us that: "A man's stomach shall be satisfied from the fruit of his mouth; From the produce of his lips he shall be filled. Death and life are in the power of the tongue, and those who love it will eat its fruit." The tongue can kill and the tongue can bring life. James 3:2 and 5 further tell us that: "For we all stumble in many things. If anyone does not stumble in word, he is a perfect man, able also to bridle the whole body. Even so the tongue is a little member and boasts great things." See how great a forest a little fire kindles? The man and the woman who doesn't stumble in tongue can create as God created.

Speaking is so important that even Jesus taught us to say the right thing. In Mark 11:22-24: "So Jesus answered and said to them, "Have faith in God. For assuredly, I say to you, whoever says to this mountain, 'Be removed and be cast into the sea,' and does not doubt in his heart, but believes that those things he says will be done, he will have whatever he says. Therefore I say to you, whatever things you ask when you pray, believe that you receive them, and you will have them."

In verse 22, Jesus starts by saying: Have faith in God and then he describes how we must have faith. He says if you say something, and believe that what you say will be done, then you will have what you say. Speaking is so important that it describes our faith. Faith is made up of what we say. So what have we been saying? This is not just about the things we say during our time of prayer but it's about what we are saying everyday about our lives, our future, the promises of God, what we want and what we don't want. If what we say is so important, then we should pay more attention to it and less to what we feel and think because, what we say influences how we feel and think.

You will have what you say. As soon as you figure this out, you will change what you say. You will only say what God says about you. The bible says you will have what you say but the question is, what have you been saying? More importantly, what will you be saying after reading this portion of the book? The bible is clear - you will have what you say. If you don't like what you have, change what you have been saying.

5 FAITH

In Mark 11, Jesus does the very same thing that God the Father did in Genesis 1. He cursed the Fig Tree and walked away and then the very next day the Fig Tree had withered. It's the same principle that God used, He spoke into creation and what He spoke became, with no time delay. Jesus is demonstrating to us what being made in the image and likeness of God really means. For Jesus it wasn't a one-time thing: 1) The blind saw as soon as He spoke; 2) The lame picked up their mats and walked; 3) The woman with the issue of blood was healed immediately; 4) The demon possessed man in the tomb was freed; 5) The son who had fits and fell into the fire was delivered; and 6) Lazarus was raised from the dead. Jesus was in the business of doing exactly what God the Father did, He spoke things and there was no process, no time delay, things happened exactly as he spoke them.

Mark 11:22 tells us that our faith must be in God. That is where the power of the process lies. Believe. Our faith is not in the process, a method or in an event. Our faith is in God. Even though Abraham and Sarah were old, they believed the One who promised more than they believed their old bodies. We also must reach a point where we believe God more than the doctor's report or the bank balance i.e. more than the situation we see, hear, and feel. We must believe God.

So why must we believe God?

✓ Let us hold fast the declaration of our hope without wavering, for He who promised is faithful. (Hebrews 10:23)

✓ For all the promises of God in Him are yes, and in Him Amen, to the glory of God through us. (II Corinthians 1:20)

✓ Then the Lord said to me, "You have seen well, for I am ready to perform my word." (Jeremiah 1:12)

✓ "For My thoughts are not your thoughts, nor are your ways my ways," says the LORD. "For as the heavens are higher than the earth, so are my ways higher than your ways, and my thoughts than your thoughts. "For as the rain comes down, and the snow from heaven, And do not return there, But water the earth, And make it bring forth and bud, That it may give seed to the sower And bread to the eater, So shall My word be that goes forth from My mouth; It shall not return to Me void, But it shall accomplish what I please, And it shall prosper in the thing for which I sent it. (Isaiah 55:8-11)

✓ I will worship toward Your holy temple, And praise Your name For Your loving-kindness and Your truth; For You have magnified Your word above all Your name. (Psalms 138:2)

We believe God because of what He says about Himself in His Word. The Word of God is above our experiences and instead of reducing who God is to our experiences, we must always elevate Him to the level of His word and in time our experiences will rise to the level of the word.

When you believe who God is, then you pray from a place of peace. Isaiah 26:3 and 4 says: "You will keep him in perfect peace, Whose mind is stayed on You, Because he trusts in You. Trust in the Lord forever, For in YAH, the Lord, is everlasting strength." When you pray, you must pray from a position of peace, you can't afford to panic or to be desperate. If we trust God, then we know that He will do what He said He would do.

Hebrews 4:2 instructs us to mix the words that we hear with faith for it to profit us. For indeed, the gospel was preached to us as well as to them; but the word which they heard did not profit them, not being mixed with faith in those who heard it. We cannot ask ourselves: what if God doesn't answer? Because faith says He will and when we know that He will answer, then we have peace. Philippians 4:6-7 articulates it ever so perfectly when it instructs us to: "Be anxious for nothing, but in everything by prayer and supplication, with thanksgiving, let your requests be made known to God; and the peace of God, which surpasses all understanding, will guard your hearts and minds through Christ Jesus."

Faith is a principle which ensures that we do not just operate in the natural. Faith makes us go beyond the limitations of time and the natural processes that govern life and enter the realm that Jesus and God the Father operate in. The bible says in Hebrews 11:1-3 and 6: "Now faith is the substance of things hoped for, the evidence of things not seen. For by it the elders obtained a good testimony. By faith we understand that the worlds were framed by the Word of God, so that the things that are seen were not made of things that are visible. But without faith it is impossible to please Him, for he who comes to God must believe that He is, and that He is a rewarder of those who diligently seek Him."

Repeatedly the Word of God brings us back to a place of faith. Faith is our way of life: For we walk by faith, not by sight. (II Corinthians 5:7) and Hebrews 10:38 tells us that: "The just shall live by faith." Faith is not just something we use when we pray but it is how we walk and how we live.

6 THE WORD

It is difficult to follow someone when you can't hear what they are saying or when they are just quiet. It is just as difficult to follow someone you refuse to listen to. The reason one listens is that it is important to know what the leader says about where we are going. When Jesus called the disciples, he made it clear where He was taking them. He told them they were going to be turned into fishers of men. From that day forward the disciples walked with and listened to Christ, and over time His words turned them into the fishers of men he wanted them to become. Jesus was doing exactly what God did in the beginning. God has blessed us with His written word, for us to be able to know what is it that he thinks about us, to communicate what He expects from us and what we can expect from Him.

The word of God is able to create from nothing. God's word has the power to create and cause lives to significantly change. It is the word from the mouth of God that is able to turn things around for the better. It is therefore in our best interest to be certain that what we hear and believe is from God.

Ezekiel 3:1-5 says; Moreover He said to me, "Son of man, eat what you find; eat this scroll, and go, speak to the house of Israel." So I opened my mouth, and He caused me to eat that scroll. And He said to me, "Son of man, feed your belly, and fill your stomach with this scroll that I give you." So I ate, and it was in my mouth like honey in sweetness. Then He said to me: "Son of man, go to the house of Israel and speak with My words to them.

When we spend time reading the Word of God we are able to transform our own lives and moreover we are able to teach others and positively influence their lives. We are never going to be able to teach what we don't know. That is why The Lord said to Ezekiel before he goes to talk to the Israelites he had to eat the scroll first and feel his stomach with it. It is the word of God that we have internalised that we speak and it changes lives. The bible says out of the abundance of the heart the mouth shall speak. Before our mouths can speak the word, the word needs to find its way into our hearts. This makes regular studying and meditating on the word important.

So why must we spend time in the word?

✓ Your word is a lamp to my feet And a light to my path.(Psalms 119:105)

✓ How can a young man cleanse his way? By taking heed according to your word. With my whole heart I have sought you; oh, let me not wander from your commandments! Your word I have hidden in my heart, that I might not sin against you. (Psalms 119:9-11)

✓ And you shall know the truth, and the truth shall make you free." (John 8:32)

✓ So shall My word be that goes forth from My mouth; It shall not return to Me void, But it shall accomplish what I please, And it shall prosper in the thing for which I sent it. (Isaiah 55: 11)

✓ This Book of the Law shall not depart from your mouth, but you shall meditate in it day and night, that you may observe to do according to all that is written in it. For then you will make your way prosperous, and then you will have good success. (Joshua 1:8)

✓   These were more fair-minded than those in Thessalonica, in that they received the word with all readiness, and searched the Scriptures daily to find out whether these things were so. (Acts 17:11)

✓   But be doers of the word, and not hearers only, deceiving yourselves. For if anyone is a hearer of the word and not a doer, he is like a man observing his natural face in a mirror; for he observes himself, goes away, and immediately forgets what kind of man he was. But he who looks into the perfect law of liberty and continues in it, and is not a forgetful hearer but a doer of the work, this one will be blessed in what he does. (James 1:22-25)

✓   All Scripture is given by inspiration of God, and is profitable for doctrine, for reproof, for correction, for instruction in righteousness, (2 Timothy 3:16)

The word is good enough to teach, to rebuke and to instruct. As we read and do the word, we increasingly become like Christ. The creative power of the word transforms us into the image of God. The image we lost when Adam sinned. That image is contained in its perfect form, in the word. The more we regain our likeness and image, the easier it gets to use the word of God to create. To speak the word with our mouths on a daily basis, whether it is in prayer or regular conversations.

The above scriptures teach that we need to know the word. We need to know what God is saying to and about us. This will ultimately help us with what we say to God when we engage in prayer. The word makes it easier for us to know how to approach God and what to approach Him for. We are not going to find ourselves asking for things that we already have. When we know what the word is saying, we will declare the word in faith and wait for God to perform it.

SECTION B: PRAYER DECLARATIONS

7 IDENTITY

When I was younger, my family had a small Norfolk terrier dog named Tiki. Tiki was a very friendly dog but he was also a very cheeky dog, especially when males were walking past our house. Tiki would bark at every boy or man that passed our house and chase them endlessly. The people who were being chased would run as fast as they could but on a few occasions, the people that Tiki was chasing would turn back and pretend as if they were chasing Tiki. When confronted, Tiki would scream out of fear and immediately run back home.

A lot of people ran away from Tiki because they just assumed that Tiki would bite them, but they never really knew that they were more powerful than Tiki and that actually, Tiki was the one afraid of them. It is the exact same with most of us. We go through life afraid of things that are afraid of us because we don't know ourselves. If you don't know yourself, you will run away from things that should be running away from you.

Most of us think about who we are according to our past. Human nature thinks in terms of trends and we are conditioned to predict our future behaviour and present conditions by our past behaviour. The Word of God turns our beliefs on their heads, in that it says: forget who you are now and who you have been in the past but instead read the word and let it introduce you to who you really are. As you read the Word of God, who you are is revealed to you.

The verses and declarations that follow are the start of that journey of introducing you to who you truly are. For those of you who already know who you truly are, these verses and declarations will serve as a reminder of your identity. As you continue to speak out loud who God says you are, you are also agreeing with heaven and who you truly are will be established in your spirit.

16

Theme verse: identity

Then God said, "Let Us make man in Our image, according to Our likeness; let them have dominion over the fish of the sea, over the birds of the air, and over the cattle, over all the earth and over every creeping thing that creeps on the earth." So God created man in His own image; in the image of God He created him; male and female He created them. Then God blessed them, and God said to them, "Be fruitful and multiply; fill the earth and subdue it; have dominion over the fish of the sea, over the birds of the air, and over every living thing that moves on the earth. (Genesis 1: 26-28)

Supporting verses: identity

✓ You are of God, little children, and have overcome them, because He who is in you is greater than he who is in the world. (I John 4:4)

✓ Yet in all these things, we are more than conquerors through Him who loved us. (Romans 8:37)

✓ For "who has known the mind of the LORD that he may instruct Him?" But we have the mind of Christ. (I Corinthians 2:16)

✓ Love has been perfected among us in this: that we may have boldness in the Day of Judgment; because as He is, so are we in this world. (I John 4:17)

✓ If then you were raised with Christ, seek those things which are above, where Christ is, sitting at the right hand of God. Set your mind on things above, not on things on the earth. For you died, and your life is hidden with Christ in God. When Christ who is our life appears, then you also will appear with Him in glory. (Colossians 3:1-4)

Declarations: Identity

I am made in the image of God
I am made according to the likeness of God
I am created according to the likeness of God
I reject low self-esteem because I am made in the image of God
I have been given dominion by God in the name of Jesus
I have dominion in the workplace, in business, in my studies, in my family and in every situation I face
Circumstances do not dominate me
I walk in dominion at all times
I am blessed by God
I am a man or a woman of God
I am anointed in Jesus' name
I am destined to be great
I am called
I am called to serve in the kingdom of God
For I am made in the image of God
I am made according to the likeness of God

I am saved
I am washed by the blood of Jesus Christ
I am redeemed
I am bought with a price
My life is not my own
And I am made in the image of God
I am made according to the likeness of God

I am fruitful in every area of my life
I multiply in all I do
I am blessed to be fruitful and to multiply
I fill the earth and I subdue it
I have dominion in the name of Jesus
For I am made in the image of God
I am made according to the likeness of God

I am of God
I have overcome the world
I have already overcome in the name of Jesus
I am walking in victory
I am not afraid because greater is He that is in me than the one that is in the world
I am made in the image of God
I am made according to the likeness of God

I do not doubt myself because my confidence is in Christ Jesus
I am going out there to build great things because I serve a great God
My mind is set on the kingdom of God
I have the mind of Christ
No problem is too difficult for me in the name of Jesus
As Christ is, so am I in this world
For I am made in the image of God
I am made according to the likeness of God

I am raised with Christ
I seek the things which are above, where Christ is
I set my mind on things above and not on things on the earth
My life is hidden with Christ in God
No harm can come upon me because I am hidden in Christ
I am raised up together with Christ and I'm sitting in the heavenly places in Christ Jesus
I am made in the image of God
I am made according to the likeness of God

I speak over my life and I declare that my life will align with the Word of
God
I am who God says that I am in the name of Jesus
I am who the Word of God says that I am
I believe who the Word of God says I am
My circumstances do not define me but the Word of God defines me
My identity is not in circumstances my identity is in the Word of God
My identity is in God
For I am made in the image of God
I am made according to the likeness of God

The Word of God is above every circumstance in my life
The Word of God is the final authority in my life
The Word of God is changing my circumstances
The Word of God is changing my situation
The Word of God is changing my life
I am made in the image of God
I am made according to the likeness of God

Jesus, thank you for my identity
My identity is in Christ Jesus
The Word of God reveals who I am
I have a revelation of who I am in the name of Jesus
I am made in the image of God
I am made according to the likeness of God

8 PURPOSE

Dr Myles Munroe famously said: "Where purpose is not known, abuse is inevitable." Many of us are wasting our lives because we don't have the WHY for our lives. We spend our days watching other people, thinking they are the ones who deserve to be great and not us, and miss out on our purpose.

We can only be wildly successful when we begin to live lives that are aligned to the purpose of God. We understand the concept of purpose when we consider a fish trying to run on land or a bird being measured on its ability to do geometry. This concept must help us understand that if we are fish, then we are designed to swim and if we are birds, then we must fly. Your genius will be revealed as soon as you align all your earthly efforts with the purpose and will of God for your life.

The Word of God keeps introducing us to people who never thought they could amount to much, who couldn't see themselves outside of their circumstances until they came into contact with the Word of God. The only way that we are ever going to understand why we are here on earth, is when we look at ourselves through the mirror of the Word of God.

Every person has a purpose and it's not something reserved for some special people. Every purpose is important and no one must feel they have an inferior purpose. These declarations will establish you in what God has called you for and remind you that you are not alone in achieving that purpose. When you meet challenges, remember you are called for such a time as this.

Theme verse: Purpose

Then the word of the LORD came to me, saying: "Before I formed you in the womb I knew you; before you were born I sanctified you; I ordained you a prophet to the nations." (Jeremiah 1:4-5)

Supporting verses: Purpose

✓ For You formed my inward parts; You covered me in my mother's womb. I will praise You, for I am fearfully and wonderfully made; Marvellous are Your works, And that my soul knows very well. Your eyes saw my substance, being yet unformed. And in Your book, they all were written, the days fashioned for me, when as yet there were none of them. (Psalms 139:13-14, 16)

✓ I, therefore, the prisoner of the Lord, beseech you to walk worthy of the calling with which you were called, with all lowliness and gentleness, with long-suffering, bearing with one another in love, endeavouring to keep the unity of the Spirit in the bond of peace. (Ephesians 4:1-3)

✓ Therefore, if anyone cleanses himself from the latter, he will be a vessel for honour, sanctified and useful for the Master, prepared for every good work. (II Timothy 2:21)

✓ The steps of a good man are ordered by the Lord, And He delights in his way. Though he fall, he shall not be utterly cast down; For the Lord upholds him with His hand. (Psalms 37:23, 24)

✓ But you are a chosen generation, a royal priesthood, a holy nation, His own special people, that you may proclaim the praises of Him who called you out of darkness into His marvellous light; who once were not a people but are now the people of God, who had not obtained mercy but now have obtained mercy. (I Peter 2:9-10 NKJV)

✓ For if you remain completely silent at this time, relief and deliverance will arise for the Jews from another place, but you and your father's house will perish. Yet who knows whether you have come to the kingdom for such a time as this. (Esther 4: 14 NKJV)

Declarations: Purpose

God knew me before I was formed in my mother's womb
I was chosen before I was born
I did not come to earth by accident or by mistake
I am sanctified and set apart by God in the name of Jesus
I was ordained to the nations
I am born for a reason
God has already called and sanctified me for His work

God covered me in my mother's womb
I am fearfully and wonderfully made
I am the work of God
The work of God is marvellous
I am marvellous
I am special
I am anointed in the name of Jesus
I am called
For God knew me before I was formed in my mother's womb
I was chosen before I was born

God knew me before I was formed in my mother's womb
I was chosen before I was born
God saw me before I was formed
All my days were written in the book of God
My days were fashioned by God before I started my life on earth
My days are on purpose
My days were designed by God
My days were predetermined by God

I walk worthy of my calling
My walk does not bring shame to my calling
My steps are ordered by the Lord
I am always guided by God
I never walk alone
I am sanctified in the name of Jesus
I am set apart for the work of God
For God knew me before I was formed in my mother's womb
I was chosen before I was born

I am a vessel of honour
I am sanctified and useful for God, my Master
I am prepared by God for every good work
I do not serve out of my own strength or intelligence
I am prepared by God for this work
I am a vessel of honour in the name of Jesus
God knew me before I was formed in my mother's womb
I was chosen before I was born

The Lord has established us as a holy people to Himself
I am are a royal priesthood
I am chosen in the name of Jesus
I am holy
I am God's own special person
I proclaim the praises of God
For God knew me before I was formed in my mother's womb
I was chosen before I was born

I am the righteousness of God, I am made righteous by the blood of the lamb
I am a citizen of the kingdom of God
It gives my heavenly Father pleasure to give me the kingdom
I am co-heir with Jesus Christ
I am a co-worker with God in the name of Jesus
All I do in the kingdom of God is mixed with faith
I am a soul winner
I bring the lost back to God
God knew me before I was formed in my mother's womb
I was chosen before I was born

I am living in my purpose
Every day I am getting closer and closer to my purpose and destiny
Everything that I need for my purpose is being added into my life
The purpose of God will not fail in my life
The purpose of God is being fulfilled in my life
My father calls and equips
I am equipped for my purpose in the name of Jesus
For God knew me before I was formed in my mother's womb
I was chosen before I was born

Lord I thank you that I know my purpose
My purpose is revealed to me in the name of Jesus
My purpose brings glory to God
My purpose glorifies the name of the Lord
For God knew me before I was formed in my mother's womb
I was chosen before I was born

God knew me before I was formed in my mother's womb
I was chosen before I was born
I was born for such a time as this
I am in the kingdom for this time and this season
I will not be silent in the name of Jesus
I thank God that I am born at this time
No one has to do what I am born to do
For I am here and I was born for such a time as this

9 AUTHORITY

You may have witnessed a traffic officer on duty, controlling traffic at a busy intersection. The traffic officer's job includes controlling multi-ton tankers and trucks much larger than the officer. The ability to control these vehicles, to tell them to stop or to move, is not based on strength and size, but authority. The authority of this officer comes from the state. The tankers and the trucks stop because they know that if they don't, they will have to account to the state. What matters is therefore the ability of the state to enforce the law and not the size or strength of the officer. It's the authority of the state that the officer therefore relies on.

I have been on a busy intersection where a volunteer decided to direct traffic when the lights were out. In this case, the motorists obey the volunteer only because they choose to, but they have no obligation to obey because the volunteer has no authority to perform traffic duties. The volunteer is performing the exact same duties a uniformed officer would but has no authority. We must not approach our position as children of God in the spiritual realm as if we are volunteering. We have been given authority to enforce order, we are the uniformed traffic officers that God has entrusted with His power.

Situations we have authority over continue to dominate us because we do not know our own power. We don't know that we have the power to command those situations to listen to us and change.

Authority is not courage based on our abilities but authority is given by God and no one can take from us what God has already given us. You don't have to feel the authority, all you need to do is believe. When you take your place of authority it may appear that nothing is happening but if God says you have the authority, then you believe even when you see, feel, and hear nothing.

Don't be afraid of appearing silly when you speak to things that in the natural seem not to hear. Taking authority is a spiritual principle must be observed as such.

Theme verse: Authority

Behold, I give you the authority to trample on serpents and scorpions, and over all the power of the enemy, and nothing shall by any means hurt you. (Luke 10:19)

Supporting verses: Authority

✓   And when He had called His twelve disciples to Him, He gave them power over unclean spirits, to cast them out, and to heal all kinds of sickness and all kinds of disease. Heal the sick, cleanse the lepers, raise the dead, cast out demons. Freely you have received, freely give. (Matthew 10:1, 8)

✓   But you shall receive power when the Holy Spirit has come upon you; and you shall be witnesses to Me in Jerusalem, and in all Judea and Samaria, and to the end of the earth." (Acts 1:8)

✓   And Jesus came and spoke to them, saying, "All authority has been given to Me in heaven and on earth. Go therefore and make disciples of all the nations, baptizing them in the name of the Father and of the Son and of the Holy Spirit, teaching them to observe all things that I have commanded you; and lo, I am with you always, even to the end of the age." Amen. (Matthew 28:18-20)

✓   And the LORD said to Abram, after Lot had separated from him: "Lift your eyes now and look from the place where you are— northward, southward, eastward, and westward; for all the land which you see I give to you and your descendants forever. Arise, walk in the land through its length and its width, for I give it to you." (Genesis 13:14-15, 17)

Declarations: Authority

Jesus has given me authority
My authority is from above and no one can take it from me
I have authority over all the power of the enemy in the name of Jesus
Nothing shall by any means harm me
I trample over scorpions and serpents
I have authority over sickness and disease
I have authority over lack and poverty
I have authority over bondage, oppression and all the powers of the kingdom of darkness

I have been given power
I have power over unclean spirits
I cast out unclean sprits in the name of Jesus
I have been given power to heal all kinds of diseases and sicknesses
For I have authority over all the power of the enemy
Nothing shall by any means harm me

The Holy Spirit is upon me
The Holy Spirit has given me power to witness for Jesus on the earth
I do ministry by the power of the Holy Spirit
I do not rely on my power
I do not rely on my expertise and experience
I rely totally and wholly upon the power of the Holy Spirit
I have authority to make disciples for Jesus
I have authority over all the power of the enemy
Nothing shall by any means harm me

I lift up my eyes from where I am
I lift up my eyes from my circumstances
I look to the South, to the East and to the West
As far as I can see the land is mine
God has given me the land I see
God has given me the land I walk on
I have authority over all the power of the enemy
Nothing shall by any means harm me

I exercise my authority in the name of Jesus
I walk in my authority
I speak into the atmosphere
I exercise my authority in the spiritual realm
For I have authority over all the power of the enemy
Nothing shall by any means harm me

I do not keep silent
I speak from a place of authority
I speak to nations in the name of Jesus
I speak to our generation and generations to come
I speak order and the manifestation of the Word of God
I declare the fulfillment of the Word of God in our generation

10 THE ANOINTING

It is believed that the origin of the concept of anointing is from a popular practice of shepherds. It is said that pests and other insects would trouble the sheep to the extent that they could burrow through the sheep's ear into the head and kill the sheep. So, shepherds would pour oil onto the sheep's head, which would make the wool slippery and thus impossible for the pests to go near the ears of the sheep as they would slide off. Anointing therefore became a symbol of protection and empowerment.

During biblical times, people were anointed with oil to signify God's blessing, empowerment, and call upon that person's life. We all need the anointing because it empowers and enables us to work in the kingdom. The anointing must never be reduced to gimmicks, or eliciting of excitement - it is so much more than that. The anointing is for breaking the curse of poverty, to heal the broken-hearted and to free those who are oppressed and bound.

There are things that we can only be able to do if we operate under the anointing. The anointing must never be limited to a time of ministry within the bounds of the four walls of a house of worship during a church service. We must always live our lives being empowered by the anointing as we perform our kingdom assignments. Without the anointing the work of the kingdom becomes difficult.

When I was a student in high school, we took typing classes. I'm not sure if there were no computers but in my school we only used typewriters. The kind of typewriter we used was the type that you had to put in paper, and pull a lever to go to the next line. If you made a mistake you had to take the page out and start afresh on a new page. I was the worst student in the typing class. The Catholic Nun that was in charge of the class kept shouting with a Belgian accent: "Pertunia (my so-called Christian name), stop looking at your fingers!"

I hated that class. I just wasn't fast enough, I couldn't type without looking at my fingers. I made so many mistakes that I spent the whole period starting at the top of the page.

To me, the anointing is just like the introduction of a computer, especially after years of struggling with the typewriter. I no longer had to worry about paper, starting afresh and physically pulling levers. I just pressed the enter button to go to the next line and I simply pressed the delete button to deal with errors. Typing finally became enjoyable, I could focus on the purpose of typing and finishing a report or assignment.

The anointing empowers us in the same way. It frees us from worrying about the mechanics and allows us to focus on our mission. When you are laying hands on the sick, the anointing says you don't have to worry about how the healing will come. When you preach you don't need to concern yourself about changing the lives of people. The anointing does all that for you. Don't continue using your typewriter when the anointing gives you access to a powerful computer. Tap into the anointing and allow the power of God to take you to a level you could never reach without the anointing.

Theme verse: The anointing

The Spirit of the LORD is upon Me, Because He has anointed Me To preach the gospel to the poor; He has sent Me to heal the broken-hearted, To proclaim liberty to the captives And recovery of sight to the blind, To set at liberty those who are oppressed; To proclaim the acceptable year of the LORD." (Luke 4:18-19)

Supporting verses: The anointing

✓ But the anointing which you have received from Him abides in you, and you do not need that anyone teach you; but as the same anointing teaches you concerning all things, and is true, and is not a lie, and just as it has taught you, you will abide in Him. (I John 2:27)

✓ Now, He who establishes us with you in Christ and has anointed us is God, (II Corinthians 1:21)

✓ It shall come to pass in that day That his burden will be taken away from your shoulder, And his yoke from your neck, And the yoke will be destroyed because of the anointing oil. (Isaiah 10:27)

✓ And my speech and my preaching were not with persuasive words of human wisdom, but in demonstration of the Spirit and of power, that your faith should not be in the wisdom of men but in the power of God. (I Corinthians 2:4-5)

✓ And Samuel said to Jesse, "are all the young men here?" Then he said, "There remains yet the youngest, and there he is, keeping the sheep." And Samuel said to Jesse, "Send and bring him. For we will not sit down till he comes here." So he sent and brought him in. Now he has ruddy, with bright eyes, and good-looking. And The Lord said, "Arise, anoint him: for this is the one!" Then Samuel took the horn of oil and anointed him in the midst of his brothers; and the Spirit of The Lord came upon David from that day forward. So Samuel arose and went to Ramah. (1 Samuel 16:11-13)

✓   So I said: "woe is me, for I am undone! Because I am a man of unclean lips, and I dwell in the midst of a people of unclean lips, for my eyes have seen the King, The Lord of hosts". Then one of the Seraphim flew to me, having in his hand a live coal, which he had taken with the tongs from the altar. And he touched my mouth with it and said: "Behold, this has touched your lips, your iniquity is taken away and your sin purged." Also, I heard the voice of The Lord saying: "whom shall I send, and who will go for Us?" Then I said, "Here am I! send me." (Isaiah 6:5-8)

Declarations: The anointing

Jesus is the anointed one
The same anointing that is upon Jesus is operating in my life
I am anointed
The spirit of God is upon me
I am anointed to preach the gospel in the name of Jesus
I am anointed to heal the broken-hearted
I am anointed to proclaim liberty to the captives
I am anointed to proclaim recovery of sight to the blind

I am empowered by the spirit of God to do kingdom works in the name
of Jesus
I am anointed by the spirit of God to do my kingdom assignment
The anointing teaches me
The anointing teaches me concerning all things
The anointing speaks the truth
The anointing does not lie
I am anointed
The spirit of God is upon me

The anointing is breaking every yoke in my life
I am anointed to break every yoke of the enemy in the name of Jesus
The anointing is removing every burden in my life
I am anointed to remove every burden in the name of Jesus
I am free in the name of Jesus
I set other people free in the name of Jesus
The anointing empowers me to set the captives free in Jesus' name
For I am anointed
The spirit of God is upon me

I am a leader in my field
For I am anointed for it
I am chosen by God, for a specific purpose
And I am anointed for it
I am sanctified for my calling
I am enabled for my calling

I am empowered for my kingdom assignment
For I am anointed
And the Spirit of God is upon me

I don't use human wisdom in the kingdom
I am empowered by the spirit of God
I am followed by signs and wonders
I don't follow signs and wonders
I don't rely on my abilities, but the spirit of God
For I am anointed
The spirit of God is upon me

I am saved by the son of God
I am established by God
I am anointed by the spirit of God
I agree to be sent by God
For I am anointed
The spirit of God is upon me

I am anointed
The spirit of God is upon me
I thank God for the anointing upon my life
I thank God that I am anointed
The anointing upon my life brings God glory
I am the anointed of God in the name of Jesus

11 THE CHURCH

The church is an institution that was created by Jesus Christ Himself. Jesus is the Head of the Church and the Church is the body of Christ. It is important for us as Christians to understand why God set up the church so that we can always run it the way He wanted. The Church belongs to God and the only way to run it, is God's way. When the church is healthy, it empowers and builds the Christian, it is a light to a lost and hurting world, and it accomplishes the mission of God on the earth.

When we pray for our local churches, we should never focus on what is happening in the church. The devil has been working to discredit the church and often our prayers as believers have been full of us describing the situation in our churches back to God.

When you are tempted to describe how bad things are at your church or in another church that you know about, just take these declarations and begin to speak over that church. We are going to transform our churches by just speaking over them and restoring them back to their original place and purpose. In our meetings as church members, let us agree together and lead one another with these declarations.

I have been a pastor for some time now. One of the things that I find painful is when I meet someone who has not known love, who has lived a life that has known nothing but pain. I have met a number of people who come to church and immediately or gradually find a place of love and peace, a sense of family, and a sanctuary of healing and deliverance. After a painful and difficult life, people young and old meet God and find the church, and a chapter they never knew existed opens right in front of them.

The church has a special place in all of our lives, nothing can replace it, and as children of God we must guard it and make sure others also experience this power.

Theme verse: The Church

And I also say to you that you are Peter, and on this rock I will build by church, and the gates of hades shall not prevail against it. I will give you the keys of the kingdom of heaven and whatever you bind on earth will be bound in heaven and whatever you loose on earth with loosed in heaven. (Matthew 16:18-19)

Supporting verses: The Church

✓ To the intent that now the manifold wisdom of God might be made known by the church to the principalities and powers in the heavenly places. (Ephesians 3:10)

✓ Now you are the body of Christ, and members individually. And God has appointed these in the church; first apostles, second prophets, third teachers, after that miracles, then gifts of healings, helps, administrations, varieties of tongues. (1 Corinthians 12: 27-28)

✓ And He Himself gave some to be apostles, some prophets, some evangelists, and some pastors and teachers, for the equipping of the saints for the work of ministry, for the edifying of the body of Christ, till we all come to the unity of the faith and of the knowledge of the Son of God, to a perfect man, to the measure of the stature of the fullness of Christ; that we should no longer be children, tossed to and fro and carried about with every wind of doctrine, by the trickery of men, in the cunning craftiness of deceitful plotting, but, speaking the truth in love, may grow up in all things into Him who is the head—Christ— from whom the whole body, joined and knit together by what every joint supplies, according to the effective working by which every part does its share, causes growth of the body for the edifying of itself in love. (Ephesians 4:11-16)

✓   There are diversities of gifts, but the same Spirit. There are differences of ministries, but the same Lord. And there are diversities of activities, but it is the same God who works all in all. But the manifestation of the Spirit is given to each one for the profit of all: for to one is given the word of wisdom through the Spirit, to another the word of knowledge through the same Spirit, to another faith by the same Spirit, to another gifts of healings by the same Spirit, to another the working of miracles, to another prophecy, to another discerning of spirits, to another different kinds of tongues, to another the interpretation of tongues. But one and the same Spirit works all these things, distributing to each one individually as He wills. For as the body is one and has many members, but all the members of that one body, being many, are one body, so also is Christ. (I Corinthians 12:4-12)

✓   "Then I heard a loud voice saying in heaven: Now salvation, and strength, and the kingdom of our God, and the power of His Christ have come, for the accuser of our brethren, who accused them before our God, day and night, has been cast down. And they overcame him by the blood of the Lamb and by the word of their testimony, and they did not love their lives to the death." (Revelation 12: 10-11)

✓   "Then the seventh angel sounded: And there were loud voices in heaven, saying, "The kingdoms of this world have become the kingdoms of our Lord and of His Christ, and He shall reign forever and ever!" (Revelation 11:15)

Declarations: The church

Jesus Himself builds the church
The gates of Hell shall not prevail against the church
The church has the keys on the kingdom of heaven
Whatever I bind on earth will be bound in heaven
Whatever I loose on earth will be loosed in heave in the name of Jesus
The church is the body of Christ
And I am a member of the body of Christ
The church belongs only to Jesus who is the Head of the Church and the Great Shepherd
As the church, we are taking back our authority

The church is the body of Christ
And I am a member of the body of Christ
Jesus Himself appoints the fivefold ministry
Jesus appoints apostles, prophets, evangelists, pastors, and teachers to equip the church
The fivefold ministry equips the church for the work of ministry
The fivefold ministry edifies the church
The fivefold ministry unites the church
The church is mature
The church is growing into Christ, the Head
Every member of the church is engaged in their kingdom assignments
Every member of the church is effective and playing their part

I am an active member of the church of Jesus Christ
The church is edified by my service
The church is edified by my gift
The church is edified by my anointing
I am a blessing to the church and the church is a blessing to me
The church is the body of Christ
And I am a member of the body of Christ

The church is the body of Christ
And I am a member of the body of Christ
All the gifts that are operating in the church are from the Spirit of God
No strange spirits are operating in the church
We silence and stop all strange spirits that are operating in the church

The word of wisdom is operating in the church
The word of knowledge is operating in the church
Faith is operating in the church
Gifts of healings are operating in the church
The working of miracles are operating in the church
Prophecy is operating in the church
Discerning of spirits is operating in the church
Different kinds of tongues are operating in the church
The interpretation of tongues is operating in the church

The spirit of God distributes as He wills
I receive what has been distributed to me
I am faithful with my gift
All of us in the church are members of one body, the body of Christ
The church is the body of Christ
And I am a member of the body of Christ

The church is the body of Christ
And I am a member of the body of Christ
The church overcomes the devil by the blood of the Lamb and the word
of our testimony
The church makes known the wisdom of God
The church is not weak
The church is strong
The church overcomes
The kingdom of our God, and the power of His Christ have come
Until the kingdoms of this world become the kingdoms of our Lord and
of His Christ, Jesus shall reign forever and ever.

I thank God that the church is the body of Christ
And I am a member of the body of Christ
I thank God for the leadership of the church
I thank God for everyone that serves in the church
I speak a blessing upon everyone who builds the church
I declare a special blessing on all who build the church

12 THE BLESSING

Jesus' most famous sermon is the Beatitudes. Jesus spends the first eleven verses of this sermon describing what the blessing is. To me, this is the strangest definition of blessed people I've ever seen. Jesus says, the poor in spirit are blessed, those who mourn, the meek, those who hunger and thirst for righteousness, the merciful, the pure in heart, the peacemakers and those who are persecuted; these are the ones Jesus called blessed. In his sermon, Jesus continues to tell us why they are blessed: they shall inherit the kingdom of God, be comforted, inherit the earth, be filled, obtain mercy, see God, and be called the sons of God.

We must understand what the blessing is so that we don't get fooled and so that we can recognise the true blessing when it comes into our lives. We are blessed because God Himself blessed us. We are not blessed because of our position or possessions, but we are blessed because God has blessed us and what God has blessed will remain blessed forever.

As we declare and command the blessing, we set a spiritual law in motion. The law that says you shall decree a thing and it will be established for you and you shall have what you say.

The blessing is more than just things, the blessing may get you things or it may give you peace as you wait for things. What you have and what you do not have doesn't change the fact that you are blessed. Blessed people transcend material things because they have something greater than material possessions. Don't downgrade the blessing by reducing it to stuff; the blessing is so much more than that.

Theme verse: The Blessing

Then God blessed them, and God said to them, "Be fruitful and multiply; fill the earth and subdue it; have dominion over the fish of the sea, over the birds of the air, and over every living thing that moves on the earth. (Genesis 1:28)

Supporting verses: The Blessing

✓ Blessed be the God and Father of our Lord Jesus Christ, who has blessed us with every spiritual blessing in heavenly places in Christ Jesus. (Ephesians 1:3)

✓ All these blessings shall come upon you and overtake you, because you obey the voice of the Lord your God. (Deuteronomy 28: 2)

Blessed shall be the fruit of your body, the produce of your ground and the increase of your herds, the increase of your cattle and the offspring of your flocks. "Blessed shall be your basket and your kneading bowl. "Blessed shall you be when you come in, and blessed shall you be when you go out. "The LORD will cause your enemies who rise against you to be defeated before your face; they shall come out against you one way and flee before you seven ways." The LORD will command the blessing on you in your storehouses and in all to which you set your hand, and He will bless you in the land which the LORD your God is giving to you. "The LORD will establish you as a holy people to Himself, just as He has sworn to you, if you keep the commandments of the LORD your God and walk in His ways. Then all peoples of the earth shall see that you are called by the name of the LORD, and they shall be afraid of you. And the LORD will grant you plenty of goods, in the fruit of your body, in the increase of your livestock, and in the produce of your ground, in the land of which the LORD swore to your fathers to give you. The LORD will open to you His good treasure, the heavens, to give the rain to your land in its season, and to bless all the work of your hand. You shall lend too many nations, but you shall not borrow. And the LORD will make you the head and not the tail; you shall be above only, and not be beneath, if you heed the commandments of the LORD your God, which I command you today, and are careful to observe them. So you shall not turn aside from any of the words, which I command you this day, to the right or the left, to go after other gods to serve them. (Deuteronomy 28:3-14)

✓   Grace and peace be multiplied to you in the knowledge of God and of Jesus our Lord, as His divine power has given to us all things that pertain to life and godliness, through the knowledge of Him who called us by glory and virtue, by which have been given to us exceedingly great and precious promises, that through these you may be partakers of the divine nature, having escaped the corruption that is in the world through lust. (II Peter 1:2-4)

✓   Therefore, I also, after I heard of your faith in the Lord Jesus and your love for all the saints, do not cease to give thanks for you, making mention of you in my prayers: that the God of our Lord Jesus Christ, the Father of glory, may give to you the spirit of wisdom and revelation in the knowledge of Him, the eyes of your understanding being enlightened; that you may know what is the hope of His calling, what are the riches of the glory of His inheritance in the saints, and what is the exceeding greatness of His power toward us who believe, according to the working of His mighty power which He worked in Christ when He raised Him from the dead and seated Him at His right hand in the heavenly places, far above all principality and power and might and dominion, and every name that is named, not only in this age but also in that which is to come. And He put all things under His feet, and gave Him to be head over all things to the church, which is His body, the fullness of Him who fills all in all. (Ephesians 1:15-23)

✓   The blessing of the LORD makes one rich, And He adds no sorrow with it. (Proverbs 10:22)

Declarations: The blessing

I am blessed by God Himself
I was blessed in the beginning at creation
I am blessed to be fruitful and to multiply
I am blessed to fill the earth and subdue it
I am blessed with every spiritual blessing in heavenly places in Christ Jesus

All the blessings from God shall come upon me and overtake me because I obey the voice of the Lord
I am blessed in the city
I am blessed in the country

The fruit of my body is blessed in the name of Jesus
The produce of my ground is blessed
The increase of my herds is blessed
The increase of my cattle and the offspring of my flocks are blessed
My basket and my kneading bowl is blessed
I am blessed when I come in, and blessed when I go out
I am blessed by God Himself in the name of Jesus
I was blessed in the beginning at creation
I am blessed to be fruitful and to multiply
I am blessed to fill the earth and subdue it

I am blessed by God Himself
I was blessed in the beginning at creation
I am blessed to be fruitful and to multiply
I am blessed to fill the earth and subdue it
The LORD causes my enemies who rise against me to be defeated before my face
My enemies shall come out against me one way and flee before me seven ways in the name of Jesus
The LORD will command the blessing on me in my storehouses
God will command the blessing in all to which I set my hand
God will bless me in the land that He is giving me
The LORD will establish me as a holy people to Himself in the name of Jesus
By Grace, I keep the commandments of the LORD and I walk in His ways
All the peoples of the earth shall see that I am called by the name of the LORD

I am blessed by God Himself
I was blessed in the beginning at creation
I am blessed to be fruitful and to multiply
I am blessed to fill the earth and subdue it
The LORD will grant me plenty of goods, in the fruit of my body, in the increase of my livestock, and in the produce of my ground, in the land that the LORD gives me
The LORD will open to me His good treasure, the heavens, to give the rain to my land in its season, and to bless all the work of my hand

I shall lend to many nations, but I shall not borrow
The LORD will make me the head and not the tail

I shall be above only, and not be beneath
I heed the commandments of the LORD my God, and I am careful to observe them
I shall not turn aside from the Word of God, to the right or the left, to go after other gods to serve them
God's divine power has given to me all things that pertain to life and godliness
I am blessed by God Himself
I was blessed in the beginning at creation
I am blessed to be fruitful and to multiply
I am blessed to fill the earth and subdue it

I have everything that pertains to life and godliness
I have the blessing of the Lord, the blessing that adds no sorrow
There is no sorrow in my blessing
The blessing of the Lord makes me rich
The blessing goes ahead of me and paves the way
The blessing makes me rich with finances, in my soul and in my spirit
I am rich with finances
I am rich with relationships
I am rich in my soul
I am rich in my spirit
I am rich because of the blessing and I have no sorrow
I am blessed by God Himself
I was blessed in the beginning at creation
I am blessed to be fruitful and to multiply
I am blessed to fill the earth and subdue it

13 GIFTS & TALENTS

In the parable of the talents, the master gives his servants his money. He then tells them to do business until he comes back. When he comes back he asks all of them to come and account for the talents he gave them. He congratulates and appreciates the two servants who doubled what he had given them, but he is upset with the one who buried his talents and had nothing to show for what he was given. The servant did not lose the talent or reduce it, he just kept it as he had received it and because of that he was called wicked.

To use our talents is not optional, we must all use our talents and gifts because the God who has given them to us, will one day require us to come and account for it. Sometimes life discourages us and tells us that our gifts do not measure up, but these declarations remind us to keep pushing until we are also able to multiply what the Master has given us.

If I get my bonus at work and give it to my sister to go and donate it to a charity for me, and she decides that the money is not enough and she then keeps it because she is too embarrassed to give it to the charity, that makes her a thief. That money was never hers, it was mine and I chose to give it to a charity. We are clear about how wrong this is, but we are not as clear when it comes to our gifts and talents. Those gifts and talents were given to us by God to edify and bless the church, they are not ours to keep and look down on. Every time when you feel like you have nothing to offer the world, just remember that the gift is from God and He gave it to you for the church, it is not yours.

May these declarations give us boldness to express every gift and talent that God has given us. May we rise from the ashes and from complacency to glorify God with every gift.

Theme verse: Gifts and Talents

For I would that all men were even as I myself. But every man hath his proper gift of God, one after this manner, and another after that. (1 Corinthians 7:7)

Supporting verses: Gifts and Talents

✓ 'For to everyone who has, more will be given, and he will have abundance; but from him who does not have, even what he has will be taken away. (Matthew 25:29)

✓ A man's gift maketh room for him, and bringeth him before great men. (Proverbs 18:16 KJV)

✓ Then the Lord answered me and said: "Write the vision and make it plain on tablets, that he may run who reads it. For the vision is yet for an appointed time; But at the end it will speak, and it will not lie. Though it tarries, wait for it; because it will surely come, it will not tarry. (Habakkuk 2:2, 3)

✓ Do you see a man who excels in his work? He will stand before kings; He will not stand before unknown men. (Proverbs 22:29)

✓ For I know the thoughts that I think toward you, says the Lord, thoughts of peace and not of evil, to give you a future and a hope. (Jeremiah 29:11)

✓ But as it is written: "Eye has not seen, nor ear heard, nor have entered into the heart of man the things which God has prepared for those who love Him." (I Corinthians 2:9)

✓ But the manifestation of the Spirit is given to each one for the profit of all. (I Corinthians 12:7)

✓ As each one has received the gift, minister it to one another, as good stewards of the manifold grace of God. (I Peter 4:10)

✓ Having then gifts differing according to the grace that is given to us, let us use them: if prophecy, let us prophesy in proportion to our faith; or ministry, let use it in our ministering; he who teaches, in teaching; he who exhorts, in exhortation; he who gives, with liberality; he who leads, with diligence; he who shows mercy, with cheerfulness. (Romans12:6-8)

Declarations: Gifts and Talents

I am a gift in the kingdom
I am multiplying my gift
I have my proper gift of God
I am faithful with what God has given me and therefore more is given to me
I have abundance in the name of Jesus
I am faithful with my gift
I am faithful with my calling
My gift makes room for me and brings me before great people
When my gift elevates me, I remain humble
I excel in my work and therefore, I stand before kings
God gives me a future that I hope for

No eye has seen, no ear has heard and it hasn't entered into the heart of man the things that God has prepared for me
I am faithful with my talents, my time and my gifts
God is giving me cities in the name of Jesus
I am a faithful servant in the house of God
I am a gift in the kingdom
I am multiplying my gift
My gift is for the profit of all
My gift benefits the body of Christ
I minister to others as I have been given the gift
I am a good steward of my gift in the name of Jesus

I am a gift in the kingdom
I am multiplying my gift
I use my gift to spread the gospel
Until the nations of this world become the nation of my God
I declare salvation and deliverance in the name of Jesus
I proclaim and I declare that sinners are coming into the kingdom of God
I pray to The Lord of the harvest: raise workers, raise labourers for the kingdom of God
I am ready to serve in the kingdom

I am serving in the name of Jesus

My desire is to do the will of my Father
It gives me great pleasure to serve in the kingdom
I serve out of love
I am anointed to serve
I am anointed to work
I am a co-labourer with Christ Jesus
I am faithful with little and therefore, God has entrusted me with much
I am a gift in the kingdom
I am multiplying my gift

I believe that the Holy Spirit is at work in my life
Signs follow me because I believe
In the name of Jesus I cast out demons
I speak with new tongues in the name of Jesus
I take up serpents; and if I drink anything deadly, it will by no means hurt me
I lay hands on the sick, and they recover in the name of Jesus
I am a gift in the kingdom
I am multiplying my gift

The Holy Spirit has come upon me
I have received power in the name of Jesus
I am a witness to Jesus in my country and continent and to the end of the earth.
I am anointed for greater works
I am the chosen of God in the name of Jesus
I am a gift in the kingdom
I am multiplying my gift

I am a gift in the kingdom
I am multiplying my gift
I am called of God
I am of God
I have overcome the world in the name of Jesus
I am more than a conqueror
I can do all things through Christ who can strengthen me

Greater is he that is in me than He that is in the world
I have everything that pertains to life and godliness
My needs are met according to God's riches in glory
I am anointed to serve

I am a gift in the kingdom
I am multiplying my gift
I am gifted
I am anointed in the name of Jesus
I am called of God
I am principled
I am a man/woman of God
I know God and therefore, I do great exploits for Him
I am led by the Spirit of God
I am a visionary
God's plan for my life is prevailing
I am going higher and higher in Christ Jesus

Our gifts differ according to the grace that is given to us
I prophecy in proportion to my faith
I use my ministry for ministering
I use my teaching gift to teach in the name of Jesus
I exhort with my gift
I give liberally in the name of Jesus
I lead with diligence
I show mercy with cheerfulness
I am a gift in the kingdom
I am multiplying my gift

I am a gift in the kingdom
I am multiplying my gift
I thank God for all my gifts
I thank God for all my talents
I am blessed to be gifted and talented in this manner

14 BUILDING

If you walk past a construction site, it's often difficult to see what is being built, especially when you don't have the blueprint or the plan. At the beginning of a building project, most of us just see confusion. Holes are being dug, trucks are moving, people are drawing and having discussions, some are mixing concrete, and if you don't have the master-plan you think it is chaos but the master-builder knows exactly what he is doing. The fact that we can't see what is being built does not mean anything, the builder knows what he is doing; the potter knows what he is creating.

There are so many things that we are building: our lives, families, ministries, businesses, dreams, etc. In this entire process of building we need to stand on the sure foundation of the Word of God. You may not have the master-plan but God, the master-builder, knows and He is in control.

As children of God we are building what God has already designed. We don't build according to our own desires and plans. The plan for what we are building is laid out in the bible and declaring the bible is the best way to build. At times, we don't even know what God is building in our lives, but we need to trust His flawless record; whatever he starts He completes.

One verse that really intrigues me in the bible is Isaiah 45:9 and it will be worthwhile to look at it in a number of versions:

NKJV- "Woe to those who quarrel with their Maker, those who are nothing but potsherds among the potsherds on the ground. Does the clay say to the potter, 'What are you making?'

CEV- "The Lord said: Israel, you have no right to argue with your Creator. You are merely a clay pot shaped by a potter. The clay doesn't ask, "Why did you make me this way? Where are the handles?"

ERV- "Look at these people! They are arguing with the one who made them. Look at them argue with me. They are like pieces of clay from a broken pot. Clay does not say to the one molding it, 'Man, what are you doing?' Things that are made don't have the power to question the one who makes them."

Our human nature may want answers but we must always remember that we are the clay and the potter is the one that is in charge. We put our faith in the Potter and we must allow Him to mold us as he sees fit.

Theme verse: Building

Therefore, whoever hears these sayings of mine, and does them, I will liken him to a wise man who built his house on the rock: and the rain descended, the floods came, and the winds blew and beat on that house; and it did not fall, for it was founded on the rock. (Matthew 7:24-25)

Supporting verses: Building

✓ As you therefore have received Christ Jesus the Lord, so walk in Him, rooted and built up in Him and established in the faith, as you have been taught, abounding in it with thanksgiving. (Colossians 2:6-7)

✓ According to the grace of God, which was given to me, as a wise master builder I have laid the foundation, and another builds on it. But let each one take heed of how he builds on it. For no other foundation can anyone lay than that which is laid, which is Jesus Christ. (I Corinthians 3:9-11)

✓ Coming to Him as to a living stone, rejected indeed by men, but chosen by God and precious, you also, as living stones, are being built up a spiritual house, a holy priesthood, to offer up spiritual sacrifices acceptable to God through Jesus Christ. But you are a chosen generation, a royal priesthood, a holy nation, His own special people, that you may proclaim the praises of Him, who called you out of darkness into His marvellous light; who once were not a people but are now the people of God, who had not obtained mercy but now have obtained mercy. (I Peter 2:4-5, 9-10)

Declarations: building

I am a wise builder
God has given me the grace to build
I am a hearer of the Word of God
I am a doer of the Word of God
I am wise because of the Word of God
I have built my house on the rock in the name of Jesus
Jesus is the rock of my salvation

My house is founded on the rock of my salvation, which is Jesus Christ
The house of my ministry is founded on the rock
The house of my family is founded on the rock
The house of my business is founded on the rock
The house of my career is founded on the rock
The house of my studies is founded on the rock
The rain can descend, the winds can blow and beat my house, but it will not fall in the name of Jesus
I am a wise builder
God has given me the grace to build

I am a wise builder
God has given me the grace to build
I build on the foundation that was laid, which is Jesus Christ
I reject any foundation that is not Jesus Christ
I reject all false religion and strange spirits in the name of Jesus
What I build is from generation to generation
What I build outlives me
I take heed how I build
I build on the foundation that was laid, which is Jesus Christ
I come to Jesus, the living stone
I am also a living stone
I am being built up as a spiritual house

I am a wise builder
God has given me the grace to build
My life will never be the same again
The way I build will never be the same again
I build by the Word of God
I build in the Word of God
I build through the Word of God
Everything that was made, is made by the Word of God
I build in love

I spend time in the Word of God
I spend time with the Word of God
The Word of God is my compass
The Word of God is a lamp unto my feet
The Word of God is a light unto my path
To build with God is an honour
To build in God is a privilege
I thank God in the name of Jesus
I am a wise builder
God has given me the grace to build

15 SPIRITUAL WARFARE

Consider what would happen if you find yourself at the Olympic Games and you happen to be on the track for the 800m race but you don't know why you are there or even that the games are on. You think you are just taking a walk but actually you are representing your country. The gun goes off and you just keep walking. All the other athletes run past you. You are in a race but you just don't know.

Maybe you are on a battlefield. Bullets are being fired at you but you don't even know that you are at war. Just because you don't know that you are in a war, it doesn't mean that the bullets will forgive you. The bullet won't say: "He doesn't understand that he is in a war so let me just excuse him and not kill him." The bullet will hit you, whether you know about the war or not.

Whether you know it or not, we are all in a spiritual war. The fact that you choose to be passive in this war will never exempt you from being attacked and even killed. Our spiritual war is real and our enemy is also very real.

Theme verse: Spiritual Warfare

"When you go out to battle against your enemies, and see horses and chariots and people more numerous than you, do not be afraid of them; for the LORD your God is with you, who brought you up from the land of Egypt. So it shall be, when you are on the verge of battle that the priest shall approach and speak to the people. And he shall say to them, 'Hear, O Israel: Today you are on the verge of battle with your enemies. Do not let your heart faint, do not be afraid, and do not tremble or be terrified because of them; for the LORD your God is He who goes with you, to fight for you against your enemies, to save you." (Deuteronomy 20:1-4)

Supporting verses: Spiritual Warfare

✓ So he answered, "Do not fear, for those who are with us are more than those who are with them." And Elisha prayed, and said, "Lord, I pray, open his eyes that he may see." Then the Lord opened the eyes of the young man, and he saw. And behold, the mountain was full of horses and chariots of fire all around Elisha. (II Kings 6:16, 17)

✓ Finally, my brethren, be strong in the Lord and in the power of His might. Put on the whole armour of God that you may be able to stand against the wiles of the devil. For we do not wrestle against flesh and blood, but against principalities, against powers, against the rulers of the darkness of this age, against spiritual hosts of wickedness in the heavenly places. Therefore, take up the whole armour of God that you may be able to withstand in the evil day, and having done all, to stand. Stand therefore, having girded your waist with truth, having put on the breastplate of righteousness, and having shod your feet with the preparation of the gospel of peace; above all, taking the shield of faith with which you will be able to quench all the fiery darts of the wicked one. And take the helmet of salvation, and the sword of the Spirit, which is the Word of God; praying always with all prayer and supplication in the Spirit, being watchful to this end with all perseverance and supplication for all the saints. (Ephesians 6:10-18)

✓   For though we walk in the flesh, we do not war according to the flesh. For the weapons of our warfare are not carnal but mighty in God for pulling down strongholds, casting down arguments and every high thing that exalts itself against the knowledge of God, bringing every thought into captivity to the obedience of Christ, and being ready to punish all disobedience when your obedience is fulfilled. (II Corinthians 10:3-6)

✓   So shall they fear The name of the Lord from the west, And His glory from the rising of the sun; When the enemy comes in like a flood, The Spirit of the Lord will lift up a standard against him. (Isaiah 59:19)

✓   In righteousness you shall be established; You shall be far from oppression, for you shall not fear; And from terror, for it shall not come near you. Indeed, they shall surely assemble, but not because of Me. Whoever assembles against you shall fall for your sake. "Behold, I have created the blacksmith Who blows the coals in the fire, Who brings forth an instrument for his work; And I have created the spoiler to destroy. No weapon formed against you shall prosper, And every tongue, which rises against you in judgment You shall condemn. This is the heritage of the servants of the Lord, And their righteousness is from Me," says the Lord. (Isaiah 54:14-17)

✓   So it was, whenever the ark set out, that Moses said: "Rise up, O Lord! Let Your enemies be scattered, And let those who hate You flee before You." And when it rested, he said: "Return, O Lord, To the many thousands of Israel." (Numbers 10:35, 36)

✓   Let God arise, Let His enemies be scattered; Let those also who hate Him flee before Him. (Psalms 68:1)

Declarations: Spiritual Warfare

My heart is not faint
I am not afraid in the name of Jesus
I do not tremble
I am not terrified because of my enemies
The LORD my God is He who goes with me
God fights for me against my enemies, to save me
I do not fight against flesh and blood in the name of Jesus

I walk by faith
I do not walk by sight
What I believe is greater than what I see
I do not fight against flesh and blood in the name of Jesus
I never fight against people
I fight against principalities in the name of Jesus
I fight against powers in the name of Jesus
I fight against the rulers of the darkness of this age
I fight against spiritual hosts of wickedness in the heavenly places

I fight the fight of faith, and therefore I always win
I am more than a conqueror in Christ Jesus
I am strong in The Lord and in the power of His might
I am putting on the whole armour of God in the name of Jesus

My waist is girded with the belt of truth
Every lie that is said against me cannot prevail because I am wearing the belt of truth
All conspiracies against me shall not succeed because I am wearing the belt of truth
I do not fight against flesh and blood in the name of Jesus

I do not fight against flesh and blood in the name of Jesus
I put on the breastplate of righteousness
I am the righteousness of God
The blood of Jesus makes me righteous
The breastplate of righteousness protects and covers my heart
Righteousness protects my heart from unbelief
Righteousness protects my heart from bitterness and hate

Righteousness protects my heart from hurt and pain
Righteousness covers me with the love of God
I know God loves me not because of my works but because the blood
of Jesus makes me righteous
I put on the breastplate of righteousness in Jesus' name

I do not fight against flesh and blood in the name of Jesus
My feet are fitted with the preparation of the gospel of peace
My feet are beautiful because they are bringing good news
Everywhere I go I bring good news
I am prepared to preach the gospel of peace
I am full of the Word of God
I have filled my heart, my mouth and my mind with the Word of God
The word prepares my feet for the gospel of peace
Every place I get to, I bring peace
My Lord and saviour, Jesus Christ, is the prince of peace

Above all, I am taking the shield of faith with which I will be able to
quench all the fiery darts of the wicked one
I live by faith and not by sight
My life is a life of faith
Faith protects me from all the plans of the devil
Faith is my shield that never fails
I do not fight against flesh and blood in the name of Jesus

I do not fight against flesh and blood in the name of Jesus
I put on the helmet of salvation in the name of Jesus
Salvation protects my mind
I think like Christ
I have the mind of Christ
I do not think according to my circumstances but according to the
Word of God

I do not fight against flesh and blood in the name of Jesus
I have the sword of the Spirit, which is the Word of God
I am full of the word
I fight with the word
I do not fight with my ideas or opinions

I fight by, in and through the Word of God

I pray always with all prayer and supplication in the Spirit
I am watchful with all perseverance and supplication for all the saints
I watch and pray as Jesus commanded
Prayer is my lifestyle
I am constantly in prayer
I pray without ceasing
I do not fight against flesh and blood in the name of Jesus

I cancel all generational curses in my life and I release generational blessings in the name of Jesus
I cancel every evil word that has been spoken against my life, my future, my family, my children, and my children's children
I am the righteousness of God and I leave an inheritance for my descendants
No weapon formed against me shall prosper in the name of Jesus
Every tongue raised against me shall be condemned in the name of Jesus
I do not fight against flesh and blood in the name of Jesus

I believe that Jesus Christ died for me
He rose on the third day and is seated on the right hand of the father, interceding for me
Jesus is interceding for me
I have eternal life
I have life more abundantly
I have life to its fullest
Because of the blood of Jesus, I have conquered sickness and disease
The power of the blood of Jesus is at work in my life
I decree and I declare that the blood of Jesus goes ahead of me
The blood is opening doors for me
Death cannot find me because I am covered by the blood of Jesus
I do not fight against flesh and blood in the name of Jesus

Arise oh God, and let your enemies be scattered
Let everything that contradicts the Word of God be scattered
Arise on my behalf Lord Jesus
I do not fight against flesh and blood in the name of Jesus

16 BREAKTHROUGH

My favourite definition of the word breakthrough is: a military movement or advance all the way through and beyond an enemy's front-line defense. To breakthrough is to advance all the way through and beyond. Breakthrough is active and it is not passive. We can't be timid around our breakthrough and we can't allow our enemies to walk all over us.

We don't have to wait for things to change, we can speak the change we desire into existence. Breakthrough is all about advancing and invading the enemy's camp. We must be militant and vigilant in bringing the will of God to pass in our lives.

It is easy to understand robbery in the natural. If someone takes your things without your permission and without your knowledge, you already know that you have been robbed. You first knew that the things were yours and that is why when someone takes them without your permission, you are clear about the fact that what belongs to you was stolen.

You fight hard to get back what you know belongs to you. You are not apologetic about demanding back what is yours and you do not give up easily because you understand that anything less would be injustice. In the spiritual you must know what belongs to you. You must fight for your breakthrough because you know what God has already promised and given you. You fight knowing that these things already belong to you.

Theme verse: Breakthrough

Daniel answered and said: "Blessed be the name of God forever and ever, For wisdom and might are His. And He changes the times and the seasons; He removes kings and raises up kings; He gives wisdom to the wise and knowledge to those who have understanding. (Daniel 2:20-21)

Supporting verses: Breakthrough

✓   "And to the angel of the church in Philadelphia write, 'These things says He who is holy, He who is true, "He who has the key of David, He who opens and no one shuts, and shuts and no one opens"; "I know your works. See, I have set before you an open door, and no one can shut it; for you have a little strength, have kept My word, and have not denied My name. (Revelation 3:7-8)

✓   "While the earth remains, seedtime and harvest, cold and heat, winter and summer, and day and night shall not cease." (Genesis 8:22)

✓   'There was a famine in the land, besides the first famine that was in the days of Abraham. And Isaac went to Abimelech, king of the Philistines. Then Isaac sowed in that land, and reaped in the same year a hundredfold; and the Lord blessed him. The man began to prosper, and continued prospering until he became very prosperous." (Gen 26:1, 12&13)

✓   "While we do not look at the things which are seen, but at the things which are not seen. For the things which are seen are temporary, but the things which are not seen are eternal." (2Cor 4:18)

✓   "Brethren, I do not count myself to have apprehended, but one thing I do, forgetting those things which are behind and reaching forward to those things which are ahead. I press toward the goal for the prize of the upward call of God in Christ Jesus." (Philippians 3:13&14)

✓   "The LORD our God spoke to us in Horeb, saying: 'You have dwelt long enough at this mountain.

✓   See, I have set the land before you; go in and possess the land which the LORD swore to your fathers—to Abraham, Isaac, and Jacob—to give to them and their descendants after them.' (Deuteronomy 1:6, 8)

Declarations: Breakthrough

I decree and I declare a new season in my life in the name of Jesus
I announce the breaking forth of a new day in every area, in every sphere, and in every dimension of my life
Behold the old has passed and the new has come

I decree and I declare a new season in my life in the name of Jesus
I declare a change of season in my life
I announce a name change
I am no longer cursed but I am now blessed and highly favoured
I am no longer a sinner but I am now the righteousness of God
I am no longer sick but I am healed, I walk in divine health in Jesus' name
I command a change of season in my life
It's a new day
I declare a new day in my life
I announce a new day in my life
I declare an end to failure, unemployment, being broke, drugs, alcohol, and a life of sin
I declare the beginning of great things in my life
I declare breakthrough and restoration
I prophesy increase, uncommon favour, and supernatural blessings upon my life
I release jobs, businesses, ministries, and projects

I am thankful to God for this day
I am thankful to God for this week
I am thankful to God for this year
I am thankful to God for this season I find myself in
The challenges have made me stronger
The gifts have blessed me

I speak to the next day and I declare the will of God upon the day in Jesus' name
I speak to my business
I speak to my job
I speak to my ministry
I speak to my studies
I speak to my projects
I speak to my finances
I speak to my family
I speak to my relationships
I command you to align to the perfect plan of God in Jesus name
I command the order of God in the name of Jesus

I declare multiplication
I declare abundance
I command doors to open
I command mountains to move out of the way
I command valley to be filled in the name of Jesus
I declare supernatural breakthrough
I proclaim miracles
I release favour in the name of Jesus
My breakthrough shall manifest in the name of Jesus
I decree and I declare a new season in my life in the name of Jesus

I have been at this place for too long
I declare that I am being promoted from this place
I am going forth to possess the land ahead of me
I am possessing everything that God has given me
My breakthrough shall manifest in the name of Jesus
I decree and I declare a new season in my life in the name of Jesus

I receive my breakthrough in the name of Jesus
I thank God for this breakthrough in the name of Jesus
God is glorified through my breakthrough in the name of Jesus
My breakthrough is manifesting in the name of Jesus
My breakthrough has come in the name of Jesus
I decree and I declare a new season in my life in the name of Jesus

17 HEALING

Believing God for your healing or for the healing of a loved one can be one of the most difficult experiences that we encounter in this life. When sick, for most of us, prayer is the last thing on our mind but it's really the most important thing we need. Most times when we are sick the temptation is to curl up and sleep and feel sorry for ourselves and will ourselves back to health.

In the physical, it makes sense to curl up and wish the sickness away but in real life and as spiritual beings we need to declare the Word of God even from our sick beds.

When we have loved ones that are sick, the temptation is to cry and be emotional about being helpless and sharing in their pain but the best thing we can do for them is to declare over them and to also declare with them.

The ministry of Jesus took healing seriously. He went about teaching and healing and even today, His ministry hasn't changed. Healing is a big deal in the kingdom and before we run to other people to get solutions about our sicknesses and diseases, let us go back to the Word of God.

Theme verse: Healing

But He was wounded for our transgressions, He was bruised for our iniquities; The chastisement for our peace was upon Him, And by His stripes we are healed. (Isaiah 53:5)

... Who Himself bore our sins in His own body on the tree, that we, having died to sins, might live for righteousness— by whose stripes you were healed. (I Peter 2:24)

Supporting verses: Healing

✓ Bless the LORD, O my soul, And forget not all His benefits: Who forgives all your iniquities, Who heals all your diseases, (Psalms 103:2-3)

✓ Or do you not know that your body is the temple of the Holy Spirit who is in you, whom you have from God, and you are not your own? For you were bought at a price; therefore glorify God in your body and in your spirit, which are God's. (I Corinthians 6:19-20)

✓ Therefore, we do not lose heart. Even though our outward man is perishing, yet the inward man is being renewed day by day. For our light affliction, which is but for a moment, is working for us a far more exceeding and eternal weight of glory, while we do not look at the things, which are seen, but at the things which are not seen. For the things, which are seen are temporary, but the things, which are not seen, are eternal. (II Corinthians 4:16-18)

✓ And the prayer of faith shall save the sick, and the Lord shall raise him up; and if he have committed sins, they shall be forgiven him. Confess your faults one to another, and pray one for another, that ye may be healed. The effectual fervent prayer of a righteous man availeth much. Elias was a man subject to like passions as we are, and he prayed earnestly that it might not rain: and it rained not on the earth by the space of three years and six months. And he prayed again, and the heaven gave rain, and the earth brought forth her fruit. (James 5:15-18 KJV)

✓ You were bought at a price; do not become slaves of men. Brethren, let each one remain with God in that state in which he was called. (I Corinthians 7:23, 24)

✓ Have you not known? Have you not heard? The everlasting God, the Lord, The Creator of the ends of the earth, neither faints nor is weary. His understanding is unsearchable. He gives power to the weak, And to those who have no might He increases strength. Even the youths shall faint and be weary, and the young men shall utterly fall, but those who wait on the Lord Shall renew their strength; they shall mount up with wings like eagles, they shall run and not be weary, they shall walk and not faint. (Isaiah 40:28-31)

✓ Then Jesus went about all the cities and villages, teaching in their synagogues, preaching the gospel of the kingdom, and healing every sickness and every disease among the people. (Matthew 9:35)

Declarations: Healing

By the stripes of Jesus I am healed
I receive my healing in the name of Jesus
By the stripes of Jesus I have already been healed
My healing has already been purchased
My healing was purchased by the blood of Jesus Christ

The price for my healing has already been paid by the Lord Jesus
I bless God
My soul blesses the Lord
The Lord heals all my diseases
There is no disease that God cannot heal
No disease is incurable or terminal with God, He heals all our diseases
By the stripes of Jesus I am healed
I receive my healing in the name of Jesus

This body is the temple of the Holy Spirit
Sickness and disease have no place in this body; the Holy Spirit already
lives here
I was bought with a price
I glorify God with my body
My body and my spirit belong to God
I am not my own
I belong to God
The God who owns me, heals my body
By the stripes of Jesus I am healed
I receive my healing in the name of Jesus

I do not look at the things, which are seen
I do not consider my feelings
I do not consider the symptoms in my body
I disregard pain
I do not look at the doctor's report
I do not look at my family's medical history
I do not consider my previous diagnosis
By the stripes of Jesus I am healed
I receive my healing in the name of Jesus

I look at the things, which are not seen
I look at the Word of God, which brings me the good news of healing
I look at Jesus who is the author and finisher of my faith
I look at the promises of God, which declares that I have already been
healed
I focus on the unseen things, which are eternal
The unseen things that testify of my healing
By the stripes of Jesus I am healed
I receive my healing in the name of Jesus

By the stripes of Jesus I am healed
I receive my healing in the name of Jesus
I am healed in Jesus' name
I have been healed in Jesus' name
I receive my healing in Jesus' name
I walk in health in Jesus' name
I walk in divine and supernatural health in Jesus' name
I walk in perfect health in Jesus' name

By the stripes of Jesus I am healed
I receive my healing in the name of Jesus
Sickness and disease have no place in my life
Sickness and disease have no place in my body
My body is already a temple for the Holy Spirit, therefore, there is no
room for sickness and disease
I speak health over my body
I speak perfect health upon my body in Jesus' name
I speak divine and supernatural health upon my body in Jesus' name

I rebuke all sickness and disease in the name of Jesus
I command sickness and disease to leave this body and this mind
I declare complete and total healing in the name of Jesus
I declare wholeness in the name of Jesus
I command perfect health
Jesus still goes about healing all sicknesses and diseases
There is no sickness that Jesus cannot heal
I am healed in the name of Jesus
By the stripes of Jesus I am healed
I receive my healing in the name of Jesus

I thank God for my healing
I thank God for divine health
I declare that I am already healed
I thank God for healing me
By the stripes of Jesus I am healed
I receive my healing in the name of Jesus

18 FINANCE & OWNERSHIP

The bible teaches that silver and gold belong to God. It goes on to say, He will shake nations to ensure that finances are made available for His kingdom. When God therefore makes financial resources available to any of us, it is for more than just our own comforts and conveniences, but more for the propagation of the gospel and for being a blessing.

Finances are just resources. Money is meant to serve us; therefore, we must understand the place of money in our lives. We are not meant to live our lives chasing or making money. We are not created to be ruled by money but we are created for dominion and we must also exercise our dominion over money and material possessions.

We need money in the Kingdom of God so that we can fulfill our kingdom mission. We must raise end-time financiers of the gospel, people who know how to make, keep, and use money. The bible speaks about money and it guides us on how to use money. To succeed with money, we must hear what God says about it and we must conduct our finances in a manner that will give him glory.

It is difficult to believe God for financial breakthrough when you are not sure what His will is about your finances and about you owning stuff. When you know the will of God, then you are able to pray with confidence.

Theme verse: Finance and Ownership

Beloved, I pray that you may prosper in all things and be in health, just as your soul prospers. (III John 1:2)

Supporting verses: Finance and Ownership

✓ Blessed be the God and Father of our Lord Jesus Christ, who has blessed us with every spiritual blessing in the heavenly places in Christ. (Ephesians 1:3)

✓ Let them shout for joy and be glad, which favour my righteous cause; And let them say continually, "Let the Lord be magnified, who has pleasure in the prosperity of His servant." (Psalms 35:27)

✓ "The Spirit of the Lord God is upon Me, Because the Lord has anointed Me To preach good tidings to the poor; He has sent Me to heal the broken hearted, To proclaim liberty to the captives, And the opening of the prison to those who are bound; (Isaiah 61:1)

✓ For you know the grace of our Lord Jesus Christ, that though He was rich, yet for your sakes, He became poor, that you, through His poverty, might become rich. (II Corinthians 8:9)

✓ And my God shall supply all your needs according to His riches in glory by Christ Jesus. (Philippians 4:19)

✓ The Lord is my shepherd; I shall not want. (Psalms 23:1)

✓ Every place that the sole of your foot will tread upon I have given you, as I said to Moses. (Joshua 1:3)

Declarations: Finance and Ownership
I prosper in all things in the name of Jesus
I am blessed with every blessing in the spiritual realm
My blessings are guaranteed
My blessing is not subject to the economy or to earthly situations

God takes pleasure in my prosperity
The gospel brings good news to the poor
The anointing brings an end to poverty in the name of Jesus
The gospel tells me that I no longer have to be poor
Though Jesus was rich, for my sake He became poor
Through His poverty, I have become rich in the name of Jesus
I prosper in all things in the name of Jesus
I am blessed with every blessing in the spiritual realm

The Lord is my shepherd, I shall not want
Jehovah Jireh provides for all my needs
I do not worry about anything
I do not worry about what to eat, what to wear, and where to stay
My Heavenly Father knows that I have a need for all these things
I do not love money but money is a tool that I use for the work of the ministry
I prosper in all things in the name of Jesus
I am blessed with every blessing in the spiritual realm

I prosper in all things in the name of Jesus
I am blessed with every blessing in the spiritual realm
The blessing of the Lord makes me rich and adds no sorrow to it
God gives me the power to get wealth
Every place that the sole of my foot treads upon is mine
I am blessed to have dominion
I am an owner
I do not have debt in my life
I do not live from paycheck to paycheck
I live in abundance
I am blessed to be a blessing

I am a nation builder
I am empowered with skill and understanding
I have revelation knowledge
I am a student of the Word of God
I prosper in all things in the name of Jesus
I am blessed with every blessing in the spiritual realm

I prosper in all things in the name of Jesus
I am blessed with every blessing in the spiritual realm
I thank God for everything I own in the name of Jesus
I thank God for provision in the name of Jesus
I thank God for finances in the name of Jesus
I don't own anything
I am simply a steward
It's an honour to be a steward in the kingdom of God in Jesus' name

19 BUSINESS

One of my all-time favourite stories tells of a child whose mother sent him to the local shop to buy 80kg of maize-meal. The child then goes to the shop and as he gets there the shopkeeper is so excited that he gives the child a lollipop for free, to demonstrate his appreciation for such a large purchase in the village. The child quickly runs home and forgets the maize-meal and the change at the shop. The child goes screaming to the mom: "Mom, look what the shopkeeper gave me for free!" The mother is not interested in the lollipop but she is asking about the maize-meal and the change. The child got too consumed by the free lollipop and forgot the real reason he went to the shop.

As children of God in business, we must not be like this child. We must not be too consumed by the money and all the additional benefits that come with running successful businesses. We have to always remember that the main purpose for us being in business remains to advance the kingdom of God.

We run successful businesses as children of God so that we can employ people who may or may not know God. As all these people see how we run business, they will then come face to face with the love of God. In business, people will know the character of God through interaction with us.

God will use business to have an encounter with some who are lost but who will never make their way to a church service. As we continue to engage in the world of business, let us never forget why God placed us there. We must excel because we serve an excellent God but we also can't be so ruthless that we fail to represent our God. Jesus must be glorified in how we conduct our business affairs.

Theme verse: Business

So he called ten of his servants, delivered to them ten minas, and said to them, 'Do business till I come.' "And so it was that when he returned, having received the kingdom, he then commanded these servants, to whom he had given the money, to be called to him, that he might know how much every man had gained by trading. And he said to him, 'Well done, good servant; because you were faithful in a very little, have authority over ten cities.' (Luke 19:13, 15, 17)

Supporting verses: Business

✓　"And you shall remember the LORD your God, for it is He who gives you power to get wealth, that He may establish His covenant, which He swore to your fathers, as it is this day. (Deuteronomy 8:18)

✓　He who tills his land will be satisfied with bread, But he who follows frivolity is devoid of understanding. (Proverbs 12:11)

✓　Be diligent to know the state of your flocks, And attend to your herds; For riches are not forever, Nor does a crown endure to all generations. When the hay is removed, and the tender grass shows itself, And the herbs of the mountains are gathered in, The lambs will provide your clothing, And the goats the price of a field; You shall have enough goats' milk for your food, For the food of your household, And the nourishment of your maidservants. (Proverbs 27:23-27)

✓　There is desirable treasure, And oil in the dwelling of the wise, But a foolish man squanders it. (Proverbs 21:20)

✓　With your wisdom and your understanding You have gained riches for yourself, And gathered gold and silver into your treasuries; By your great wisdom in trade you have increased your riches, And your heart is lifted up because of your riches." (Ezekiel 28:4-5)

Declarations: Business

I am doing business until Jesus comes
I am productive in my business in the name of Jesus
I have been entrusted with talents and time
I multiply my talents and I use my time wisely
I trade wisely with everything that God has entrusted me with
I am a wise businessperson
I am faithful with the little that is entrusted to me
God will give me authority over cities

I remember the Lord my God
It is God who gives me the power to get wealth
I have the power to get wealth
I do not get wealth on my own but I have been given power
I prosper in all things in the name of Jesus
I am blessed with every blessing in the spiritual realm

I am diligent with my property
I know the state of my finances
I am an attentive businessperson
I am productive in my business
I am not lazy
I work with my hands
I do business
I am not a busy body
I am productive
I prosper in all things in the name of Jesus
I am blessed with every blessing in the spiritual realm

I prosper in all things in the name of Jesus
I am blessed with every blessing in the spiritual realm
My business is profitable
There is always a surplus in my business
I apply wisdom and understanding in my business
I have good ideas for growing the business
My business is a tool to finance the gospel
My business is a vehicle to provide the funding to reach the lost
My business is blessed by God

I speak over my business
I command it to increase
I command this business to be profitable
I declare that this business will be a blessing to all its employees
I prosper in all things in the name of Jesus
I am blessed with every blessing in the spiritual realm

I prosper in all things in the name of Jesus
I am blessed with every blessing in the spiritual realm
My business gives glory to Jesus
All who do business with me encounter the power of God
All who work for me encounter Jesus
My business is a blessing
My business is blessed in the name of Jesus

20 EMPLOYMENT

Genesis 2:5 & 15, in the New International Version, provide the best definition of work for us and it clarifies a lot of misconceptions about what work is about. The bible says: "Now, no shrub had yet appeared on the earth and no plant had yet sprung up, for the Lord God had not sent rain on the earth and there was no one to work the ground. The Lord God took the man and put him in the Garden of Eden to work it and take care of it." The first thing I understand from this scripture is that where there is a person then there is someone to work the ground. The second thing is that God put man in the garden to work it and take care of it.

This scripture confirms that for as long as we are alive, we have to work and we are placed here on earth to work. There are certain things that will never grow until we show up to work. Most people, who do not have the traditional job, consider and call themselves unemployed. Never allow unemployment to bully you into thinking you don't have work. Not being formally employed does not mean you have no work.

Don't be tempted to skip this section because you are unemployed. Ask God to reveal your work to you: begin to prophetically speak over your next workplace. As you wait on God for a place of formal employment, ask God to reveal to you what you need to work on now. What is your garden? What are some of the things that will only grow in your life as soon as you show up to work? We are dealing with employment from a spiritual point of view and not from a natural standpoint.

God will use work to make most of our dreams come true. The temptation to complain about our bosses, subordinates, salaries, working conditions, etc. will always be there, but now that we know that our words create we refuse to complain. We choose to speak over our workplaces and declare what we desire to see.

Theme verse: Employment

And Pharaoh said to his servants, "Can we find such a one as this, a man in whom is the Spirit of God?" Then Pharaoh said to Joseph, "Inasmuch as God has shown you all this, there is no one as discerning and wise as you. You shall be over my house, and all my people shall be ruled according to your word; only in regard to the throne will I be greater than you." And Pharaoh said to Joseph, "See, I have set you over all the land of Egypt." (Genesis 41:38-41)

Supporting verses: Employment

✓ Now those who are such we command and exhort through our Lord Jesus Christ that they work in quietness and eat their own bread. (II Thessalonians 3:12)

✓ Let Your work appear to Your servants, And Your glory to their children. And let the beauty of the LORD our God be upon us, And establish the work of our hands for us; Yes, establish the work of our hands. (Psalms 90:16-17)

✓ He has filled them with skill to do all manner of work of the engraver and the designer and the tapestry maker, in blue, purple, and scarlet thread, and fine linen, and of the weaver—those who do every work and those who design artistic works. (Exodus 35:35)

✓ He who has a slack hand becomes poor, But the hand of the diligent makes rich. (Proverbs 10:4)

✓ Do you see a man who excels in his work? He will stand before kings; He will not stand before unknown men. (Proverbs 22:29)

✓ The plans of the diligent lead surely to plenty, But those of everyone who is hasty, surely to poverty. The desire of the lazy man kills him, For his hands refuse to labour. (Proverbs 21:5, 25)

✓ And whatever you do, do it heartily, as to the Lord and not to men, knowing that from the Lord you will receive the reward of the inheritance; for you serve the Lord Christ. (Colossians 3:23-24)

✓ And whatever you do in word or deed, do all in the name of the Lord Jesus, giving thanks to God the Father through Him. (Colossians 3:17)

✓   He who is faithful in what is least is faithful also in much; and he who is unjust in what is least is unjust also in much. Therefore, if you have not been faithful in the unrighteous mammon, who will commit to your trust the true riches? And if you have not been faithful in what is another man's, who will give you what is your own? (Luke 16:10-12)

✓   For exaltation comes neither from the east Nor from the west nor from the south. But God is the Judge: He puts down one, And exalts another. (Psalms 75:6-7)

✓   "Enlarge the place of your tent, And let them stretch out the curtains of your dwellings; Do not spare; Lengthen your cords, And strengthen your stakes. (Isaiah 54:2)

Declarations: Employment

I have the Spirit of God
The Spirit of God is in me
God has given me a revelation of how to excel in the workplace
I have the revelation to do well in my job
I am discerning and I am wise
God has set me to occupy and to dominate in the area of my employment
I am the head in my job and not the tail
I excel in every area of my job

God has set me to occupy and to dominate in the area of my employment
I am the head in my job and not the tail
I am available to work in the area of my employment
God has placed me in this area to work
God has placed me in this organisation and in this industry to work
Multiplication and growth will occur because I am now working in this field

I declare that the work of my hands is established by God
Yes, all my efforts are established
I am filled with skill to do all the work required from me and more
God has filled me with skill to do all manner of work
Nothing is too complex or too difficult for me

I am creative, full of ideas and innovation
God has filled me with skill to do my work (mention your profession or line of work)
I am diligent in my work
The hand of the diligent makes rich and therefore I am rich
God has set me to occupy and to dominate in the area of my employment
I am the head in my job and not the tail

I excel in my work
I will not stand before ordinary men but I will stand before kings
My plans will surely lead to plenty because I am diligent
I work with all my heart because I work for the Lord
Everything I do at work I do it in the name of Jesus
Everything I do at work, I do it with thanksgiving
God has set me to occupy and to dominate in the area of my employment
I am the head in my job and not the tail

God has set me to occupy and to dominate in the area of my employment
I am the head in my job and not the tail
I am faithful with every little work that God has entrusted me with
I am faithful when no one is watching
God will entrust me with much because of my faithfulness
I am faithful with an earthly assignment
God will entrust me with an eternal assignment
I am not lazy
I work with my hands
I am not a busy body
I am productive
I am a hard worker
I am committed to my work
I declare that as I work the blessing increases in my life

I declare that I will be promoted in the name of Jesus
Promotion comes from the Lord
The Lord will promote and exalt me
God enlarges my influence in the name of Jesus
I am stretched in my responsibilities
I am ready for increase
I have prepared for increase and promotion
I do not speak against my promotion but I speak it into manifestation
I declare good things over my organisation
I speak a blessing upon my industry and sector in the name of Jesus
I declare growth and opportunities for my organisation
God has set me to occupy and to dominate in the area of my employment
I am the head in my job and not the tail

I speak over my job
I declare that my job is blessed in the name of Jesus
My job is a blessing in my life
I thank God for this job in the name of Jesus
I thank God for the opportunity to work
I thank God for the privilege to work
I command every work I engage in to be fruitful and to multiply
I thank God for this job in the name of Jesus
This job is for the glory of God in the name of Jesus
I thank God for everyone I work with in the name of Jesus
God has set me to occupy and to dominate in the area of my employment
I am the head in my job and not the tail

21 STUDIES

It is as if studies have a life of their own. For most of us who have had the privilege to study, we fully understand the challenges of the student life. The student swings between the pure bliss of student life and the horror at times of things not working out. Exams, assignments, and projects can at times take over your life, and the students who trust in God must be able to see beyond grades and marks.

When we are students, it doesn't change the fact that we are students in Christ. Being in Christ comes first and we must understand our positions more than we understand our present realities.

I arrived at Wits University to study Chemical Engineering as an A-student from High School. Up to that point in my life I had only known what it meant to excel in my studies and nothing else. My time at Wits humbled me greatly. I struggled so much with my engineering studies, to the point of despair. At some point I thought I would never graduate. At that time I didn't know what I know now. I was holding on for dear life and after much failing and crying I ultimately obtained my degree.

Every student will have their own special journey. Some will cruise through their academics; others will struggle with funding their studies, whereas some will just fail hopelessly. Regardless of what your journey is, we all need Jesus as we study. There are some who have committed suicide because they couldn't handle the pressure, others went mad, and some just abandoned the course all together. If we know the power of the Word of God to deal with our studies, then we will make these declarations. We will not only make them when things are going wrong but at all times so that God can be at the centre of our studies.

Theme verse: Studies

As for these four young men, God gave them knowledge and skill in all literature and wisdom; and Daniel had understanding in all visions and dreams. And in all matters of wisdom and understanding about which the king examined them, he found them ten times better than all the magicians and astrologers who were in all his realm. (Daniel 1:17, 20)

Supporting verses: Studies

✓ The fear of the LORD is the beginning of knowledge, But fools despise wisdom and instruction. (Proverbs 1:7)

✓ Being confident of this very thing, that He who has begun a good work in you will complete it until the day of Jesus Christ. (Philippians 1:6)

✓ Have I not commanded you? Be strong and of good courage; do not be afraid, nor be dismayed, for the LORD your God is with you wherever you go. (Joshua 1:9)

✓ But thanks be to God, who gives us the victory through our Lord Jesus Christ. Therefore, my beloved brethren, be steadfast, immovable, always abounding in the work of the Lord, knowing that your labour is not in vain in the Lord. (I Corinthians 15:57-58)

✓ For we are His workmanship, created in Christ Jesus for good works, which God prepared beforehand that we should walk in them. (Ephesians 2:10)

✓ And we know that all things work together for good to those who love God, to those who are called according to His purpose. (Romans 8:28)

✓ I can do all things through Christ who strengthens me. (Philippians 4:13)

✓ Surely goodness and mercy shall follow me All the days of my life; And I will dwell in the house of the LORD Forever. (Psalms 23:6)

✓ Have you not known? Have you not heard? The everlasting God, the LORD, The Creator of the ends of the earth, Neither faints nor is weary. His understanding is unsearchable. He gives power to the weak, And to those who have no might He increases strength. Even the youths shall faint and be weary, And the young men shall utterly fall, But those who wait on the LORD Shall renew their strength; They shall mount up with wings like eagles, They shall run and not be weary, They shall walk and not faint. (Isaiah 40:28-31)

Declarations: Studies

God has given me knowledge and skill in literature and wisdom
I am skilled in all matters of understanding and wisdom
I have knowledge because I fear and revere the Lord
God who has begun the good work of my studies will complete it
I am confident that I will finish strong

God who has begun the good work of my studies will complete it
I am confident that I will finish strong
I am not afraid because God is with me
I have victory through my Lord, Jesus Christ
I will not fail but I will pass because I have victory in the name of Jesus

I am steadfast and immovable
I abound in good works
My labour is not in vain, it will bear fruit in the name of Jesus
I am God's workmanship and I am created for good works
All things work together for my good in the name of Jesus
This course is for my good and not for my destruction
Every test, assignment, and project is working together for my good
I can do all things through Christ who strengthens me
God who has begun the good work of my studies will complete it
I am confident that I will finish strong

I am strong
I am of good courage
I am not afraid in the name of Jesus
I approach my studies with courage and by faith

I know that God is with me in everything I do
God who has begun the good work of my studies will complete it
I am confident that I will finish strong

My God never faints or sleeps
My God is watching over His Word in my life to perform it
God gives me power when I am weak in the name of Jesus
He gives me strength when I have no might
My strength is renewed because I wait on God
I will mount up with wings as an eagle
I will run and not be weary
I shall walk and not faint
God who has begun the good work of my studies will complete it
I am confident that I will finish strong

I speak over my studies
I speak success and cancel all failure in the name of Jesus
I declare that every day I am excelling in all I do
I decree that I am learning and growing
I declare that I am more confident day by day
I am increasing in wisdom and influence
I command victory in all I do in the name of Jesus
God who has begun the good work of my studies will complete it
I am confident that I will finish strong

God who has begun the good work of my studies will complete it
I am confident that I will finish strong
I am succeeding in my studies in the name of Jesus
God is providing for my studies in the name of Jesus
Jesus the provider is making everything accessible for me to study
I thank God for the opportunity to study
I thank God that my mind is healthy
I thank God that I am able to study
My studies are a blessing in the name of Jesus
I am blessed to be a student
My student life is bringing glory to God

22 MARRIAGE

The responsibility to pray for the institution of marriage doesn't only belong to the married couples but it is the responsibility of the church and society as a whole. Our nations are made up of families and when families fail, and then our nations also fail.

This section is intended to encourage all of us to go beyond praying for only our marriages but to pray for all marriages. It is also to pray for current and future marriages and to build our nations on the solid foundation of a Christ-centred family.

A strong and solid family has been the foundation of healthy lives for many people. All the enemies of marriage continue to erode that foundation and as Christians we need to arise and stand against those enemies as we build good and lasting marriages.

There was a time in our history when it was taboo to get divorced, marriages were eternal, and they lasted forever. Families were raising children in one piece and mothers and fathers were the pillar of our neighbourhoods. Somewhere, without notice, it all changed and marriage became a casualty of our busy lives and it became less important to our other, more honourable and important pursuits. We left our children to be raised by other people, we pursued money and status and now we want to choose something different. We choose to fight for the institution of marriage. We declare to build strong marriages and to frustrate every plan of the enemy to destroy marriages.

Theme verse: Marriage

And the LORD God said, "It is not good that man should be alone; I will make him a helper comparable to him." (Genesis 2:18 NKJV)

Supporting verses: Marriage

✓   Now hope does not disappoint, because the love of God has been poured out in our hearts by the Holy Spirit who was given to us. (Romans 5:5)

✓   Love never fails. But whether there are prophecies, they will fail; whether there are tongues, they will cease; whether there is knowledge, it will vanish away. (I Corinthians 13:8)

✓   But from the beginning of the creation, God 'made them male and female.' 'For this reason a man shall leave his father and mother and be joined to his wife, and the two shall become one flesh'; so then they are no longer two, but one flesh. Therefore, what God has joined together, let not man separate. (Mark 10:6-9)

✓   I will bless those who bless you, And I will curse him who curses you; And in you, all the families of the earth shall be blessed. (Genesis 12:3)

✓   For the husband is head of the wife, as also Christ is head of the church; and He is the Saviour of the body. Husbands, love your wives, just as Christ also loved the church and gave Himself for her, So husbands ought to love their own wives as their own bodies; he who loves his wife loves himself. (Ephesians 5:23, 25, 28)

✓   Let the husband render to his wife the affection due her, and likewise also the wife to her husband. The wife does not have authority over her own body, but the husband does. And likewise, the husband does not have authority over his own body, but the wife does. (I Corinthians 7:3-4 NKJV)

✓   He who finds a wife finds a good thing, And obtains favour from the LORD. (Proverbs 18:22 NKJV)

✓   Who can find a virtuous wife? For her worth is far above rubies. The heart of her husband safely trusts her; So he will have no lack of gain. (Proverbs 31:10-11)

Declarations: Marriage

As a husband,
God has made a suitable helper for me
My wife is a suitable helper to me
I love my wife as Christ loved the church
I don't love out of my own strength and might
I love out of the love of God that is shed abroad in my heart by God
I have found a good wife
And I have found favour from the Lord
I declare that marriage comes from God

As a wife,
God has made me a suitable helper for my husband
I am a suitable helper to my husband
The Holy Spirit who is our Helper as the church, teaches me to be a suitable helper
I am anointed and ordained to be a helper to my husband in the name of Jesus
I declare that marriage comes from God

I declare that marriage comes from God
My husband or my wife and I are joined together by God
We are no longer two but one flesh
We are one supernaturally in the name of Jesus
Our oneness is not physical, natural, emotional, or intellectual
Our oneness is spiritual and it is supernatural
We are made one by God

I declare that marriage comes from God
No man can separate our marriage
We declare the protection of God upon our marriage
We speak and decree the presence of God in our marriage
We come against divorce in the name of Jesus
We pray for marriages to stand
We pray for our marriage to stand
We pray for strong families

My family is blessed
My family is blessed to be a blessing
Through my family, the nations of this world will be blessed
I thank God for my marriage
I thank God that He blessed me with a partner in the name of Jesus
My marriage brings glory to God
My marriage gives hope to those who have lost hope
My marriage is used by God to be a blessing
I declare that marriage comes from God

23 CHILDREN

When God creates children, He still creates in His image and likeness. Most of us, as parents and guardians, often think we are raising children in our own image and likeness. We need to look past our problems, weaknesses and shortcomings and see children for who they really are, the image of God. We need to look at them as individuals with already established destinies, which were decided by the Father without consulting anyone. As parents, we need to acknowledge the privilege of being part of what God has already started and He Himself will complete.

The Word of God will do for our children more than what we could ever dream of as parents and guardians. It was Bishop Noel Jones who encouraged the body of Christ to pray for all children, not just our own. He asked the question: If your children are the only ones who are blessed and doing well; whose children do you think they will marry and befriend? The selfishness of praying only for our own children is actually a harm to our own selves. I would further ask: if we don't pray for all children, then do we understand that these very same children will grow up to be in positions of leadership and authority in different areas of our lives.

When children do not behave according to our desires we still need to confess what the Word of God says about them. We live in a time where children are facing giants that are much bigger than them. Giants of drugs, alcohol, sexual, physical and emotional abuse, teen pregnancy, online sexual predators, human trafficking, kidnapping, etc. The list of giants that these little people have to face is endless. As adults, we need to step in and come between the children and all the things that are trying to destroy them and steal their future. We must be vigilant in our defence of young people. We must fight because truly the children are our future. Without the children the human nation will go extinct.

During the time of Noah, God destroyed the earth with a flood because Noah's generation was wicked. We must protect our future and ensure that the next generation is not wicked. It's our responsibility to pray for the future generation so there will be a world to live in when we are old.

Theme verse: Children

Behold, children are a heritage from the LORD, The fruit of the womb is a reward. Like arrows in the hand of a warrior, So are the children of one's youth. Happy is the man who has his quiver full of them; They shall not be ashamed, But shall speak with their enemies in the gate. (Psalms 127:3-5 NKJV)

Supporting verses: Children

✓ And you, fathers, do not provoke your children to wrath, but bring them up in the training and admonition of the Lord. (Ephesians 6:4)

✓ Train up a child in the way he should go, And when he is old he will not depart from it. (Proverbs 22:6)

✓ He who spares his rod hates his son, But he who loves him disciplines him promptly. (Proverbs 13:24)

✓ He grants the barren woman a home, Like a joyful mother of children. Praise the LORD! (Psalms 113:9)

✓ And these words, which I command you today, shall be in your heart. You shall teach them diligently to your children, and shall talk of them when you sit in your house, when you walk by the way, when you lie down, and when you rise up. (Deuteronomy 6:6-7)

✓ Honour your father and your mother, that your days may be long upon the land which the LORD your God is giving you. (Exodus 20:12 NKJV)

✓ Therefore, you shall lay up these words of mine in your heart and in your soul, and bind them as a sign on your hand, and they shall be as frontlets between your eyes. You shall teach them to your children, speaking of them when you sit in your house, when you walk by the way, when you lie down, and when you rise up. (Deuteronomy 11:18-19)

✓ A good man leaves an inheritance to his children's children, But the wealth of the sinner is stored up for the righteous. (Proverbs 13:22)

Declarations: Children

Our children are a heritage from the Lord
Our children are a reward for their generation
Our children are made in the image and likeness of God
My children will not make the mistakes of their parents
My children are blessed and highly favoured

Our children are like arrows
And the Lord will shoot them into their destinies
We train our children according to the ways of the Lord
We are raising obedient children
We are raising children that will be a blessing to their generation
We are raising disciplined children
Children that bring joy to their parents
Children that honour their parents
Children that know the Word of God
Our children are made in the image and likeness of God

Our children are made in the image and likeness of God
Our children will go further than us
They will go further than the generation before them
Our children are destined for greatness, for success, and impact
We are blessed to parent our children
I am a good parent
I leave an inheritance to my children and to my children's children
My children will not start from scratch
My children will not start where I started
My children are better off

Our children are made in the image and likeness of God
I speak the protection of God upon all children
I protect children against drugs in the name of Jesus
I protect children against alcohol in the name of Jesus
I protect children against teen pregnancy in the name of Jesus
I protect children against abuse in the name of Jesus
I protect children against sexual predator in the name of Jesus
I protect children against human trafficking and kidnapping in the name
of Jesus
I declare that all children are safe in the name of Jesus
Angels are watching over the children as they play and sleep

Our children are made in the image and likeness of God
I thank God for all children
I thank God for the privilege to be a parent
I thank God to raise children for God in Jesus' name

24 BEING SINGLE

I moved from thinking that being single is a curse, to pretending that I accept being single, and then finally to this point where I completely depend on God and His perfect timing. This is the point where I have accepted that being single is fine and that I can actually be very successful leading a single life.

We find ourselves in an era of transition where family and marriage are concerned. There are many books written on the subject of getting and keeping a man or woman but very little material is found on how to live on your own and make the best of it. There are many reasons why many of us are still single or have just become single.

There are those who were just never in a relationship and no matter how much they long for and even pray for a relationship, that prayer remains unanswered and that longing unfulfilled. Much fasting and crying has gone into desiring a relationship but for some reason that elusive cupid never seems to shoot their way.

Then there are those who have loved once and just cannot bring themselves to loving again. They are convinced that the love they had is the Adam and Eve or Romeo and Juliet type and they are stuck in the past, wishing for what once was and refusing to step into the waters of relationships again. The loved one may have died, snatched by another or simply just walked away but for them, they are still stuck at the place where they disappeared into the abyss and one continues waiting in hope.

Some have been in relationships that ended and they find themselves newly single. They are disorientated because after years of living with someone they have forgotten how to live alone. Something as simple and natural as making a decision now looks like a mountain of a task because there's no one to consult and bounce ideas with.

Then there's the veteran, you have tried your hand at love many times. You hope, you pray, you do all you can and in every relationship you are sure this is the ONE but every single time it ends and you are left holding feathers while the bird is long gone. To the uninformed bystander it appears as if relationships are just a game to you because you seem to have a string of them. To the judgmental observer you may even be labeled a player but you and I know that you are giving it your all and it is just not working out.

Whatever your circumstances; they may be religious, psychological, physical, etc. these declarations are for all of us.

Being single forces you to confront yourself because you are the one person you are spending the most time with. When we were younger, we were surrounded by friends and activities but as we get older, friends are kept busy by families, young children, deaths of distant and close relatives, and if you are to live, then you have to make a choice to do certain things alone. Choose to be with God, instead of being single. Choose to spend your time in His Word: speaking and meditating on His Word.

Theme verse: Being Single

But I want you to be without care. He who is unmarried cares for the things of the Lord—how he may please the Lord. There is a difference between a wife and a virgin. The unmarried woman cares about the things of the Lord, that she may be holy both in body and in spirit. But she who is married cares about the things of the world—how she may please her husband. (I Corinthians 7:32, 34 NKJV)

Supporting verses: Being Single

✓ The LORD has appeared of old to me, saying: "Yes, I have loved you with an everlasting love; Therefore, with loving kindness I have drawn you. (Jeremiah 31:3)

✓ But now, thus says the LORD, who created you, O Jacob, And He who formed you, O Israel: "Fear not, for I have redeemed you; I have called you by your name; You are Mine. Since you were precious in My sight, You have been honoured, And I have loved you; Therefore, I will give men for you, And people for your life. (Isaiah 43:1, 4)

✓ My times are in Your hand; Deliver me from the hand of my enemies, And from those who persecute me. (Psalms 31:15)

✓ Trust in the LORD with all your heart, And lean not on your own understanding; In all your ways acknowledge Him, And He shall direct your paths. (Proverbs 3:5-6 NKJV)

✓ So teach us to number our days That we may gain a heart of wisdom. (Psalms 90:12)

✓ Keep your heart with all diligence, For out of it spring the issues of life. (Proverbs 4:23)

Declarations: Being Single

I am without care
I am a single person and I am without care
I care about the things of the Lord
I have dedicated my life to serving God
I am loved by God
I am loved with an everlasting love

I am loved by God
I am loved with an everlasting love
Being single at this point in my life is a gift
I refuse to be stressed because the times of my life are in God's hands
God is in control of everything in my life
I trust God with my whole heart
I don't lean on my own understanding
I don't depend on statistics
I'm not rushed by time
I acknowledge God in all my ways
God is directing my path
God has directed my path

I am loved
I am loved by God
I am loved with an everlasting love
The love of God towards me doesn't change
The love of God for me is sufficient
God draws me to himself
Feelings of loneliness do not drive and define me
My rest is in the love of God

God has called me by my name
I am loved by God
I am special
I have been redeemed
I have been bought with a price
I am loved by God
I am loved with an everlasting love

My season of being single is not a season of rejection
This time is precious to me and I dedicate all of it to God
Time is on my side
The owner of time is my God
My steps are ordered by the Lord
My path is directed by God
I have the grace for this time in my life
God's grace is sufficient to carry me through this time

I guard my heart with all diligence
I discern whom I allow into my heart
I am wise about who I give my heart to
I guard my heart against heartbreak and hurt
My heart belongs to God
The issues of life flow out of my heart
My heart is set on Christ
My days are filled with fulfilling the will of God
As a single person my life belongs only to God
I am loved by God
I am loved with an everlasting love

I thank God for this season of being single
I thank God for everything I am learning
I thank God for an intense time of ministry
I thank God for a time of consecration and dedication to God
I am loved by God
I am loved with an everlasting love

25 VICTORIOUS LIVING

As children of God, we are called to a life of victory. The experiences of life insist on trying to convince us that we are not winning, that we are struggling or that things are not working out for us. The truth of the matter is that we have already won, our God goes ahead of us and He fights for us and to top it off, all things work together for our good.

No matter what the current circumstance of our lives say; the Word of God confirms our victory over and over again. The Christian who knows his true identity and the contents of the bible understands that victory goes beyond our natural circumstances. Our victory is guaranteed in Jesus' name.

Theme verse: Victorious Living

But thanks be to God, who gives us the victory through our Lord Jesus Christ. (I Corinthians□ 15□:57□)

Supporting verses: Victorious Living

✓ The thief does not come except to steal, and to kill, and to destroy. I have come that they may have life, and that they may have it more abundantly. (John 10:10)

✓ Therefore, do not worry about tomorrow, for tomorrow will worry about its own things. Sufficient for the day is its own trouble. (Matthew 6:34)

✓ And the Angel of the LORD appeared to him, and said to him, "The LORD is with you, you mighty man of valor!" (Judges 6:12)

✓ Keep your heart with all diligence, For out of it spring the issues of life. (Proverbs 4:23)

✓ Finally, brethren, whatever things are true, whatever things are noble, whatever things are just, whatever things are pure, whatever things are lovely, whatever things are of good report, if there is any virtue and if there is anything praiseworthy—meditate on these things. (Philippians 4:8)

✓ I can do all things through Christ who strengthens me. (Philippians 4:13)

✓ But as it is written: "Eye has not seen, nor ear heard, Nor have entered into the heart of man The things which God has prepared for those who love Him." (I Corinthians 2: 9)

✓ For the LORD your God is He who goes with you, to fight for you against your enemies, to save you.' (Deuteronomy 20:4)

✓ What then shall we say to these things? If God is for us, who can be against us? He who did not spare His own Son, but delivered Him up for us all, how shall He not with Him also freely give us all things? Yet in all these things we are more than conquerors through Him who loved us. (Romans 8:31-32, 37)

✓ Now thanks be to God who always leads us in triumph in Christ, and through us diffuses the fragrance of His knowledge in every place. (II Corinthians 2:14)

Declarations: Victorious Living

I live in victory
I thank My God who gives me victory
I have victory in the name of Jesus
I live a life of victory
I declare and I command victory in every area of my life
I win in the name of Jesus

I declare and I command victory in every area of my life
I win in the name of Jesus
Jesus has come that I may have life
Jesus has come that I may have life more abundantly
There is abundance in my life
There's fulfillment in every area of my life
I have life to the fullest
My life is complete in Christ

I declare and I command victory in every area of my life
I win in the name of Jesus I do not worry about tomorrow
I do not worry about my future
God has already given me the victory
My victory is guaranteed in the name of Jesus

I am a mighty man of valor
I am not a weak person
I am not a defeated person
I am mighty
I am strong in the name of Jesus
I do not faint
I declare and I command victory in every area of my life
I win in the name of Jesus

I have victory in my thoughts
I think only thoughts of victory in Jesus' name
I meditate on the Word of God
I can do all things through Christ who strengthens me
Christ gives me the strength to do all things
I am strong

I declare and I command victory in every area of my life
I win in the name of Jesus

God has prepared good things for me
Eye has not seen
Ear has not heard
It has not come into the heart of men
The things that God has prepared for me
God has prepared great things for me
God has prepared marvelous and amazing things for me
I declare and I command victory in every area of my life
I win in the name of Jesus

God goes before me
God goes with me
God fights for me against my enemies in the name of Jesus
God saves me
I win in every area of my life
I declare and I command victory in every area of my life
I win in the name of Jesus

God is for me
No one can be against me
I am not alone in the name of Jesus
God has given me His Son Jesus
God has also given me all things, freely
I am more than a conqueror through God who loved me
I declare and I command victory in every area of my life
I win in the name of Jesus

God leads me in triumph in Christ
I never go forth in shame
I only go forth in triumph
I thank God for victory in the name of Jesus
I thank God for fighting for me
I am grateful for every victory in the name of Jesus
I declare and I command victory in every area of my life
I win in the name of Jesus

26 CONCLUSION

May this book provoke you to a place of prayer and to spending time in the Word of God, all the days of your life.

May these declarations move you and your congregations to a deeper place of prayer.

May corporate prayer return to our assemblies, our services, conferences, and conventions.

May no gathering of believers end without corporate prayer.

ABOUT THE AUTHOR

Mantsha Pheeha is a pastor and she has been involved in ministry for the past 20 years. She has witnessed first-hand what the Word of God can do in someone's life and she has had the privilege of seeing countless lives transform upon application of the Bible. She is a preacher and she believes firmly in the power of the Word of God to change anyone's life, regardless of the circumstances. Mantsha believes that when the church and individuals begin to have a revelation of the power of the Word of God, then miraculous transformation in all of our lives will follow.

www.ingramcontent.com/pod-product-compliance
Lightning Source LLC
Chambersburg PA
CBHW020534160726
47992CB00005BA/2382